BIBLE PRINCIPLES
for CHRISTIAN DATING

To Susan,
May this book be a blessing
To you and your family. Thank
you for your support. God has
your perfect husband on his
way. God Bless you!

BIBLE PRINCIPLES
for CHRISTIAN DATING

Douglas M. Graf

TATE PUBLISHING
AND ENTERPRISES, LLC

Bible Principles for Christian Dating
Copyright © 2013 by Douglas M. Graf. All rights reserved.

No part of this publication may be reproduced, stored in a retrieval system or transmitted in any way by any means, electronic, mechanical, photocopy, recording or otherwise without the prior permission of the author except as provided by USA copyright law.

Scripture quotations, unless otherwise indicated, are taken from the *Holy Bible, King James Version,* Cambridge, 1769. Used by permission. All rights reserved.

Scripture quotations marked (AMP) are taken from the Amplified Bible, Copyright © 1954, 1958, 1962, 1964, 1965, 1987 by The Lockman Foundation. Used by permission.

Scripture quotations marked (NIV) are taken from the *Holy Bible, New International Version*®, NIV®. Copyright © 1973, 1978, 1984 by Biblica, Inc.™ Used by permission of Zondervan. All rights reserved worldwide. www.zondervan.com

Scripture quotations marked (NLT) are taken from the *Holy Bible, New Living Translation,* copyright © 1996. Used by permission of Tyndale House Publishers, Inc., Wheaton, Illinois 60189. All rights reserved.

This book is designed to provide accurate and authoritative information with regard to the subject matter covered. This information is given with the understanding that neither the author nor Tate Publishing, LLC is engaged in rendering legal, professional advice. Since the details of your situation are fact dependent, you should additionally seek the services of a competent professional.

The opinions expressed by the author are not necessarily those of Tate Publishing, LLC.

Published by Tate Publishing & Enterprises, LLC
127 E. Trade Center Terrace | Mustang, Oklahoma 73064 USA
1.888.361.9473 | www.tatepublishing.com

Tate Publishing is committed to excellence in the publishing industry. The company reflects the philosophy established by the founders, based on Psalm 68:11,
"The Lord gave the word and great was the company of those who published it."

Book design copyright © 2013 by Tate Publishing, LLC. All rights reserved.
Cover design by Junriel Boquecosa
Interior design by Caypeeline Casas

Published in the United States of America

ISBN: 978-1-62854-332-2
1. Religion / Christian Life / Love & Marriage
2. Religion / Christian Life / Relationships
13.09.18

ACKNOWLEDGMENTS

I would like to thank my family and friends for their support and encouragement. You have all been a great help with bringing this book together, and I appreciate of all of you.

I would like to thank my pastors, Dr. Darrell Scott, Dr. Belinda Scott, and James Davis, for devoting their time into researching God's word and for their tremendous teachings. I am very thankful for my pastors who treated me with potential to grow and gave endless encouragement to me so I could be the best I can be.

And a special thanks to Dr. Mary D'Onofrio for devoting many hours proof reading and editing this book.

God bless you all.

CONTENTS

Preface 9
Preparing for a Christian Relationship 13
"The Goal" 23
The Makeup of Marriage (Adam and Eve) 29
Learning from Proverbs: Mini Sermon 39
Fellowshipping with One or Multiple People 45
The Start of Fellowshipping 47
Handling the Euphoric Phase 53
Communication 59
   Texting 62
   Communication When You Disagree 65
   Red Flag to Watch For 71
Couples Wanting Kids 73
Developing Trust 77
Being Equally Yoked 81
Prayer and Prayer for Each Other 85
Establishing Vision 93
Dating Tips and Guidelines for Safety 97

- Topics of discussion 105
- Dating with Children 117
- Interracial Dating 121
- Dating in the workplace 127
- Teenage Dating 131
- Internet Dating 135
- Don't Lead Anyone On 137
- Dating After a Bad Relationship 147
- Does Age Matter? 149
- Ending a Relationship 151
- Recovering from a Breakup 155
- Why Do You Stay? 161
- Don't Go Back 163
- Evaluating Yourself 165
- Getting Yourself Together 167
- What is Love? 173
- What the Bible says about Sex 179
- Filtering out Temptations 187
- Faith: Mini Sermon 191
- Fasting 201
- Friends and Dating 205
- Prenuptial Agreements 209
- Components to a Successful Marriage 211
- Fusion of Marriage 217
- Effects of Divorce 221
- Final Words 225

PREFACE

Have you ever wondered why some marriages last fifty- or sixty- plus years? Do you ever ask what is it that makes their marriage work or keep their marriage going? What's their secret? Well, *Bible Principles for Christian Dating* is a book that will help you with finding the love of your life, so you can be one of the marriages that people will ask: "How do you do it?"

This book gives examples of how one views fellowshipping as a friend, and how one dates to see if the other person is a potential marriage partner. You will be able to establish one of two things:

1. Are you and the other person meant to be friends and only friends?
2. Is there a strong foundation for a relationship that one wants so the relationship can last a lifetime, all of which fits within biblical guidelines?

While the Bible does not specifically address dating or how to date, this book will help you identify when you are ready to commit yourself to a person by knowing that you are ready to be exclusive with and be united to this person, in marriage for life.

Many people use different terms for what they call spending time together. I will use the terms fellowship, dating, and marriage to identify spending time together. These will be defined later.

It is important that when you are in a good, solid relationship that you are identifying your relationship with words like God, belief, comfort, confidence, commitment, compassion, companionship, courage, delight, equally yoked, faith, faithfulness, forgiveness, hope, honesty, honor, holiness, integrity, love, maturity, obedience, prayer, praise, peace, pleasure, rejoice, respect, sacrifice, righteousness, safety, sanctification, satisfaction, strength, submission, thankfulness, tithe, truth, trust, unity, understanding, and patience.

On the other hand, if words like anger, anxiety, unbelief, burden, chastisement, corruption, deception, defrauding, dishonor, disobedience, dishonesty, doubt, foolishness, haste, hate, immaturity, lust, rebellion, wickedness, and wrath characterize your relationship, it is time to move on. These words mean you are not equally yoked and/or even in danger. These words would never describe God's best for you. This is what people in secular dating/relationships put up with, not saved Christian men and women.

The following pages give many principles on relationship dating from all points of view. They will also help you learn a about yourself as well as the other person. These principles will build a foundation that can lead to a marriage that will last for a lifetime. Several different translations of the Bible have been used to illustrate the biblical reference points for easy reading. It is my intent that nothing is ambiguous to you, the reader.

WHY DO YOU NEED THIS BOOK?

1. Are you looking for a good practical approach to Christian dating?
2. Are you looking for a way to develop a strong foundation for marriage?
3. Have you ever felt used in a relationship?
4. Have you ever felt misled by someone?
5. Have you ever felt you were being treated as an object as opposed to being loved?
6. Do you ever ask yourself why can't I find a good person?
7. Do you ever ask yourself why can't I find someone who will love me and respect me?
8. Do you always seem to feel let down in your relationships?

These are all valid questions many people ask that this book will address. You can have confidence from here on that it is in God's will for you to find the perfect person in marriage, or, if you desire, the perfect person as a companion. This book will open up the scriptures for you to know and understand God's will for you.

NOTES

PREPARING FOR A CHRISTIAN RELATIONSHIP

SPENDING TIME WITH GOD

When it comes to relationships, the most important relationship you will ever have is the one between you and God. You need to spend time with God on a daily basis. You will want to find a place where the distractions will be at a minimum. Find a place where you can read your Bible, pray, praise, and worship God. This is a time that you talk to God about all your feelings, problems, desires, and vision. We will talk about this more in depth later in the book.

Why rely on God? This is a question that is easy to answer but, unfortunately, a lot of people only rely partially on God. Often people will try to work independent of God, thinking their way is fine; but when something bad happens, then they turn to God, expecting Him to straighten it out. Many people only go to God when they have problems or when they need something. God wants you to rely on him all the time, especially for making important decisions. He wants to guide your life. When you rely on God you will see His blessings come to you. Jeremiah 17:5–8 describes what the Lord says about blessings and curses when you trust in man over God.

> This is what the Lord says: "Cursed are those who put their trust in mere humans, who rely on human strength and turn their hearts away from the Lord.
> They are like stunted shrubs in the desert, with no hope for the future. They will live in the barren wilderness, in an uninhabited salty land.
> "But blessed are those who trust in the Lord and have made the Lord their hope and confidence. They are like trees planted along a riverbank, with roots that reach deep into the water. Such trees are not bothered by the heat or worried by long months of drought. Their leaves stay green, and they never stop producing fruit.
>
> Jeremiah 17:5–8 (NLT)

God wants us to rely on Him all the time, more than you know or realize. God brought his only Son (Jesus) to earth to die for us and for our sins. Jesus is our intercessor with God (Hebrews 7:25). We talk to God through Jesus. Jesus was the one who broke down every barrier for us to be able to talk to God directly.

> Therefore he is able, once and forever, to save those who come to God through him. He lives forever to intercede with God on their behalf.
>
> Hebrews 7:25–26 (NLT)

We need to delight ourselves in the Lord on a regular basis. The word *delight* means "to take pleasure in." Some people say they delight themselves in God, but they say they only read their Bible in church. It is important to understand that you cannot delight yourself in someone you do not know. The more you delight yourself in God, the more you will reflect God's character. The better the relationship you have with God, the better the relationship you will have with people. We delight ourselves in God by doing what pleases Him and putting His word in our hearts. Two scriptures that might help you with understanding how to delight yourself in God are Psalm 40:8 and Romans 7:22.

> I take joy in doing your will, my God,
> for your instructions are written on my heart."
>
> Psalm 40:8 (NLT)

> For in my inner being I delight in God's law;
>
> Romans 7:22 (NIV)

Delighting yourself in God is to know God, to love God, to please Him, and to believe in His word 100 percent.

You need to spend time with God regularly. When you spend time with God, you will become a changed person. This change will extend in all areas of your life, including how you want a Christian relationship/marriage. Your desire will become for a good Christian wife or husband. The scriptures says, "Delight thyself also in the Lord: and he shall give thee the desires of thine heart" (Psalms 37:4). You need to make your heart right first before God will provide the person for you. The scripture says: "He shall give thee the desires of thine heart." The word *desire* covers a lot and it does not mean every desire. First, if it is a selfish desire, God does not want to give it to you (but occasionally He will) because when selfish desires do not work out, we want to blame someone; some will even blame God. A selfish desire is a desire that is in the will of God, but you do not look to God for guidance for the answer. An example would be getting married. Getting married is in the will of God, but it becomes a selfish desire when you do not seek God first and only marry the person based on looks or get married impulsively. There is a satanic desire which covers all the desires that you may have that you know is not in the will of God. A satanic desire would encompass lustful acts or desires of sexual immorality. God does not bless this kind of desire at all. But the one desire that God loves to bless is a sanctified desire. This is when you desire what God desires for you. When you want what God wants, then God will truly bless you abundantly.

> But seek first his kingdom and his righteousness, and all these things will be given to you as well.
>
> Matthew 6:33 (NIV)

It is important to remember that God does not want what is good or better for you; He wants what is best for you! God wants you to be prosperous and he wants you to be healthy all the time. This also means He will provide you with a person that is the best for you. Sometimes, it may take a little time for that person to arrive or be made known to you, but God will provide.

Jesus also explains this in the New Testament about listening to Him and His teachings. He shares what the consequences would be as well.

> "Anyone who listens to my teaching and follows it is wise, like a person who builds a house on solid rock.
>
> Though the rain comes in torrents and the floodwaters rise and the winds beat against that house, it won't collapse because it is built on bedrock.
>
> But anyone who hears my teaching and doesn't obey it is foolish, like a person who builds a house on sand.
>
> When the rains and floods come and the winds beat against that house, it will collapse with a mighty crash."
>
> Matthew 7:24–27 (NLT)

By now, you can see that we need to commit ourselves to God and relying on Him for everything. As I read Psalms 37, I see that "Fret Not" is written in three places—Psalms 37:1, 37:7, and 37:8. *Fret* means "to worry." *Fret not* basically means "not to worry about things." This means when you rely on God you should not worry. Your life is in God's hands. The more you know God, the more you will love God, the more you trust God, the more you will find rest in God. The more you rest in God and wait on Him, the less you will worry about circumstances. As you trust God more, you will love Him greater. The more time you spend with God, the more you can release your worries to God because you know He is the one who will handle your circumstances.

My pastor would always tell us to read and study our Bible. Some people say they don't have time. But my pastor would make a good point saying, "If you have time to watch TV, listen to the radio, play video games, talk on your cell phone, surf the internet, etc. then you have time to read your Bible." I am very grateful for my pastors who kept reinforcing to me to read my Bible. The more I read my Bible, the more I am able to read and understand. It comes down to this—if you are going to tap into the power of God, the strength of God, and the grace of God, then you have to experience it through the word of God. Whether you are a newly converted Christian or a Christian of many years, I encourage you to find a Bible translation that is easy for you to read on a daily basis. There are also life applications Bibles that helps relate the word to your everyday circumstances. Other easier translations would be The New Living Translation, New American Standard Bible, and the New International Version, to name a few.

You may wonder how you can understand the will of God. There are three basic principles to help you understand the will of God. First, the will of God is the Bible. Everything you need to know is contained in the Bible, this includes how to live, learning experiences, and what to do and what not to do as a Christian, etc. Secondly, you have to look at the Holy Spirit as your guide. As you lean on God for direction, you will hear the Holy Spirit speak in different ways. Sometimes, you will hear His voice; sometimes, He will put a conviction on you. The conviction can be a gut feeling or something in the back of your mind saying this is not right. You will also feel a sense of confirmation or peace when something is right. Thirdly, we have to have a desire to read the Bible and listen to the Holy Spirit. If you take any one of the three things away, you will be incomplete, and may miss out on hearing God speak. Remember the Holy Spirit will never tell you to do something that goes against God's Word (the Bible).

It is important to understand that before God reveals His specific will to you, you must surrender your life to Him, as we see in Romans 12: 2. It is important to understand that the Holy Spirit will only work in your life when your body, mind, and will yields to God. You are giving your body to God, saying you are not willingly, intentionally, or deliberately sinning. Some people become saved but never get over the deliberate sins of the flesh. They feel they can sin and say God will forgive me but then turn around and deliberately sin again. The Holy Spirit does not flow through someone who neglects to listen to God's word.

> Don't copy the behavior and customs of this world, but let God transform you into a new person by changing the way you think. Then you will learn to know God's will for you, which is good and pleasing and perfect".
>
> Romans 12: 2 (NLT)

Using the word *but* when hearing from God, is almost a sure way of ignoring his will. When you hear or use the word *but*, it usually cancels what was said before it to make an excuse for what you are about to say and/or do. For example:

- If God said do not marry a certain person as you are not equally yoked, and you say, "But I'm in love," we will have time to work things out when we're married. You can see you will have a difficult marriage ahead of you.
- If God says don't talk to that person anymore, and you say, "But we're good friends," that is when your friend may bring something up unexpected in front of someone else who should not know that information. For example, if you had a problem that you were seeking help and confided into your friend when God said not to, they may bring that information up in front of your dating partner, parents, boss, etc. God knows who will be trustworthy and who will not be.
- If God says don't be by yourself with that woman or man, and you say, "But I can control myself," that is when an unexpected sexual

encounter can happen and even lead to an unexpected pregnancy and/or even a sexually transmitted disease.
- If God says tithe, and you say, "But I need lunch money; I'll just hold back $10.00," that is when you find yourself with an unexpected bill.

Every time you hear from God and you say the word *but*, you are essentially saying no to God! It is important to understand that disobedience will bring burdens. God will allow those burdens to affect you to bring you back to the blood of Jesus so he can bless you. On the other hand, if you are obedient to God's commands, God will open His blessings to you. God sees what is going on in the future and He will tell you not to go or not to do something because He is already there and knows the outcome.

You have to remember even if God tells you not to do something that you like to do and you choose to do less, doing less is still disobedience. A greater effort does not take place of obedience. An example would be the sin of premarital sex. If you are having sex on a regular basis and choose to have sex less often but not want to get delivered from the sinful nature. Less sex does not make you obedient. Trust in the Lord with all your heart. Lean on Him and not yourself. When God has your ear, He will speak to you. When He has your heart, He will minister to you. God wants what is best for us just as the loving parent who wants what is best for their kids. We just have to listen. In Psalm 32:8, God shows He will guide us, we just have to hear Him and listen. Psalms 18:30 confirms that when God says

He will guide you along the best pathway for your life, He means it because His way is perfect. This means perfect for God and perfect for you as a believer.

> The Lord says, "I will guide you along the best pathway for your life.
> I will advise you and watch over you.
>
> Psalm 32:8 (NLT)

> God's way is perfect.
> All the Lord's promises prove true.
> He is a shield for all who look to him for protection.
>
> Psalm 18:30 (NLT)

One thing that I found is that you should be connected to a good Bible-based church. You need pastors that love to dive into the word of God and have a passion for conveying it. They should also have some sort of marriage counseling or pre-marriage counseling class, whether it is the pastor himself or someone else that has been put in the role of a marriage counselor. I believe premarriage counseling is important because when you say you can do it yourself, you become prideful. A premarriage counselor will be able to identify different areas that you may need work in as a couple and will be able to give you some good advice.

"THE GOAL"

Plain and simple, what is the goal? What is it that you are trying to accomplish from dating? Are you dating just to have a companion and for friendship? Or are you dating to see if you are yoked for marriage? If you are trying to date with the intention of getting married, you should be looking for God's best for you. This means finding someone that suits you as a whole, not just in part. We call this being equally yoked. You want to find someone that has the same common interests as you and find someone that you can communicate and enjoy life with, but at the same time can be serious with.

If you find a person that has the same common interests as you, but you don't get along with them, well, that does not build a good foundation for marriage. Finding someone that you can talk with and joke around with but you have almost nothing in common does not build a good foundation either.

The purpose of this book is to bring to light many different areas in relationships so two people can properly identify characteristics of another person to see if they would be compatible for spending a lifetime together. This book will also help identify if they should remain friends but not enter into a dating relationship.

You may be a person that says you are not ready to settle down and are not sure what you want out of a relationship. This means you would be fellowshipping for friendship and not for marriage, but that needs to be clearly stated in the beginning. As you fellowship with different people, you will learn more about qualities you like in someone and the qualities you do not want in your marriage. This part of fellowshipping is definitely a platonic relationship until you determine that you are ready to date for marriage. If you are only friends with someone, then that is reciprocated by the other person as well.

If you are looking just for a companion, that is okay too! This means you are looking for someone to be friends with of the opposite sex but don't want a romantic relationship with. This type of relationship is perfectly fine. You have to make sure that this is what the other person's wishes are also. The companionship has to be mutual.

FELLOWSHIPPING

Fellowshipping in general is being friends. It's important that you communicate what your intentions are during the fellowship whether you are looking for a companion or for someone to marry. For the sake of this book, fellowshipping is broken down into two categories:

1. Spending time with someone of the opposite sex where you have the same interests as a companion with no sexual attraction.
2. Spending time with someone of the opposite sex where you try to determine if you are compatible for dating.

    - Depending on how long you have known the person, the fellowship could be exclusive from the start, saying you will not be seeking anyone else at this time, however, not committing to a serious relationship while trying to learn about them. Being exclusive does not mean you are committed. This is just a way of saying you will not shop around while you are determining if you want to date. This is the fellowship phase where you are friends. This is a personal decision and will be discussed later in this book.
    - You could also say that you are not sure you are ready to date and want to keep an open relationship in the beginning. If you have determined to not be exclusive and keep your relationship open, then this should be a short period of time. Anything long term then you should refer back to number one and let the person know you are looking more for companionship then a relationship.

DATING

The dating process is spending time with each other to determine if you are equally yoked. At this point you have determined that you are compatible on some level and are continuing to learn about each other. This is where you learn more about the other person's beliefs, likes, dislikes, habits, quirks, and responsibilities. As the dating process continues, you will share more of your life with the other person. This is where you determine if you are compatible for marriage.

MARRIAGE

The union between man and woman. This is when a man and women state their vows to one another and form a covenant between each other and with God. It is a covenant for life.

EQUALLY YOKED

This is a way of determining how well you align with the other person. Being equally yoked does not mean you do all things alike. It means you are in agreement with each other with what is going on in every phase of the relationship.

COMPANION

Someone who shares the same interests as you do but has no romantic or sexual attraction to you. They are someone that you can call and ask to go and get dinner or see a movie but no intimate quality time. A companion is a friend of the opposite sex but acts as a friend only. Some of the qualities of a companion is someone who can bring stability in your life not chaos. They are someone who will keep you encouraged. They are someone who will help add to your strength but help you through your weaknesses. They are also a good sounding board for you. You can talk about anything, and they can give honest, sound advice, even if it's something you don't want to hear but know it's good for you. They are not someone who under minds you, makes you doubt yourself, or brings up past issues or intentionally jabs at your flaws. All in all, it is good to have a companion than to be by yourself. It makes life more enjoyable and allows you to share things that bring enjoyment to you with someone else. These friends are priceless.

Often, a couple will make a marriage commitment based on very powerful romantic feelings, fueled by romantic intimacy experienced in dating, rather than a strong and healthy loving relationship based upon a solid knowledge of the Bible and each other.

THE GOAL

One thing a Christian has to remember is that they are looking for God's best for them. Sometimes it happens quickly, and sometimes it takes more time to find that right person. You need to pray and have faith in God for that person. Prayer and faith go hand in hand. You can say the best prayer on the face of the planet, but if you don't have faith, then it doesn't do you any good. This will be explained in more detail in the prayer section of this book. This is why Philippians 4:6 says, "Do not be anxious about anything, but in everything, by prayer and petition, with thanksgiving, present your requests to God." Also, let us take a look at the first part of Hebrew 12:2 where it says, "Let us fix our eyes on Jesus, the author and perfecter of our faith."

THE MAKEUP OF MARRIAGE (ADAM AND EVE)

As we take a look at the first marriage in the Bible, we can see that it was Adam and Eve. I will use this example as the base for how you, as a single person, should be looking for a spouse. There are many characteristics that you should follow when it comes to finding the right spouse. When it comes down to it, anyone can find a person of the opposite sex to marry. But it is not about who can you marry now, it is about waiting and finding the right person so we only marry once!

How do you know God wants you to be with someone? Well, let's break some scripture down. I will start in Genesis 1. In Genesis 1, you can see God creating the earth and everything in it. Here's where you start to see God's perfect work because as the days progress and God completes His work for those days, God said He saw his work and that *"it was good."*

THE MAKEUP OF MARRIAGE (ADAM AND EVE)

> And God saw the light, that *it was good*:
>
> And God called the dry land Earth; and the gathering together of the waters called he Seas: and God saw that *it was good*.
>
> And the earth brought forth grass, and herb yielding seed after his kind, and the tree yielding fruit, whose seed was in itself, after his kind: and God saw that *it was good*.
>
> And to rule over the day and over the night, and to divide the light from the darkness: and God saw that *it was good*.
>
> And God created great whales, and every living creature that moveth, which the waters brought forth abundantly, after their kind, and every winged fowl after his kind: and God saw that *it was good*.
>
> And God made the beast of the earth after his kind, and cattle after their kind, and every thing that creepeth upon the earth after his kind: and God saw that *it was good*.
>
> > Genesis 1:4, 10, 12, 18, 21, 25
> > [emphasis mine]

Then we read down to Genesis 2:18 where God *says:* "And the Lord God said, 'It is not good that the man should be alone...'" Do you see how God is working now? God could have left Adam by himself. God made everything and then said it was not good for man to be alone but then in the same verse said, "I will make him an help meet for him." This would only seem right. Let us go back to Genesis 1:21–22. In Genesis 1, God is creating everything and He tells all living things to multiply. God told every living creature to multiply. This would only make sense that God would do the same for man as well, right? I also want to point out that the first time God says something was not good is when he said it was not good for man to be alone. That says something powerful!

> And God created great whales, and every living creature that moveth, which the waters brought forth abundantly, after their kind, and every winged fowl after his kind: and God saw that it was good.
> And God blessed them, saying, Be fruitful, and multiply, and fill the waters in the seas, and let fowl multiply in the earth.
>
> Genesis 1:21-22

The Bible also shows in Proverbs 18:22 that it is good for a man to find a wife and he will obtain favor of the Lord.

> Whoso findeth a wife findeth a good thing, and obtaineth favour of the Lord."
>
> Proverbs 18:22 (KJV)

The Bible demonstrates in its first couple, Adam and Eve, that God paired them together for a lifetime. The Bible shows in Genesis 2:21-23 that a rib was taken from Adam and God formed Eve. Could God have made Eve from the soil of the earth? Absolutely! But He didn't. He made Eve from the rib of Adam so they would be reunited together as one flesh.

THE MAKEUP OF MARRIAGE (ADAM AND EVE)

> And the Lord God caused a deep sleep to fall upon Adam, and he slept: and he took one of his ribs, and closed up the flesh instead thereof;
>
> And the rib, which the Lord God had taken from man, made he a woman, and brought her unto the man.
>
> And Adam said, This is now bone of my bones, and flesh of my flesh: she shall be called Woman, because she was taken out of Man."
>
> Genesis 2:21–23

Being that Adam and Eve were the only two people on the planet, Adam did not have to go too far to find his rib. As a Christian man, we should all be seeking our rib. A man should want to find a woman that loves God as he does. A woman that can relate with him, have the desire to support him and his vision, and does not have to contest everything unnecessarily. This means even if the man says he is hearing from God to fast, the woman needs to support him. This could be by fasting herself or by supporting him while he fasts. She should be a woman that can be trustworthy and have loyalty to him. A man should be looking for his virtuous woman as described in Proverbs 31:10–31. This man is looking for his "rib"!

> A wife of noble character who can find? She is worth far more than rubies.
>
> Her husband has full confidence in her and lacks nothing of value.
>
> She brings him good, not harm, all the days of her life.

She selects wool and flax and works with eager hands.

She is like the merchant ships, bringing her food from afar.

She gets up while it is still night; she provides food for her family and portions for her female servants.

She considers a field and buys it; out of her earnings she plants a vineyard.

She sets about her work vigorously; her arms are strong for her tasks.

She sees that her trading is profitable, and her lamp does not go out at night.

In her hand she holds the distaff and grasps the spindle with her fingers.

She opens her arms to the poor and extends her hands to the needy.

When it snows, she has no fear for her household; for all of them are clothed in scarlet.

She makes coverings for her bed; she is clothed in fine linen and purple.

Her husband is respected at the city gate, where he takes his seat among the elders of the land.

She makes linen garments and sells them, and supplies the merchants with sashes.

She is clothed with strength and dignity; she can laugh at the days to come.

She speaks with wisdom, and faithful instruction is on her tongue.

She watches over the affairs of her household and does not eat the bread of idleness.

THE MAKEUP OF MARRIAGE (ADAM AND EVE)

> Her children arise and call her blessed; her husband also, and he praises her:
> "Many women do noble things, but you surpass them all."
> Charm is deceptive, and beauty is fleeting; but a woman who fears the Lord is to be praised.
> Honor her for all that her hands have done, and let her works bring her praise at the city gate.
>
> Proverbs 31:10–31 (NIV)

A man should keep in mind that this lady he is looking for may not initially appear physically as his ideal woman. When you read the scripture, there is nothing about how the woman looks! The scripture does not address how hot she is or what her figure looks like. Sure, a physical attraction starts the interest but you may find someone who suits you better that was not catching your eye to begin with. Do not limit yourself to just looks. You may be friends and develop a liking toward that person even though they may not fall in your physical ideals. This is why you need to rely on God, prayer, and an objective way of getting to know the other person (see Topics of Discussion section). You may ask yourself, "How do I hear from God or how do I rely on God?" especially if you are a new Christian or a Christian who needs more understanding. We will talk about this using Proverbs 3:5–6 later in this book.

Women need to be seeking the body they came from as well—not just seeking *a* body but *the* body she came from. First and foremost, she should be trying to find a man who will be the spiritual head of the household. She should be trying to find someone who she can relate with, a man that will provide for her, and be faithful to her. She should try to find a man that will support her as well. Now, keep in mind support does not only mean to have a house and a car. It means supporting her vision as well. He simply does the right thing at the right time, whether or not he realizes the impact his actions will have. Kind of reminds you of Boaz (See the book of Ruth). Another quality he should display is leadership qualities. If a problem occurs, does he say, "Let us find a way to solve the problem," or does he want to fault someone for what happened?

Boaz not only did what was right, he also did it the right away. At that time, he could not comprehend or even dream of all that his actions would accomplish. He did not know nor could have known that the child he would have by Ruth would be an ancestor of David and, ultimately, Jesus our Lord and Savior. He only met the challenge of taking the right action at the right time in the situation facing him.

A woman should be trying to find a man like Boaz that makes good choices, not just for himself, but can make good choices for his family. She should identify with him, his vision, and want to be submissive to him as Ephesians 5:21–30 shows:

> Submitting yourselves one to another in the fear of God.
> Wives, submit yourselves unto your own husbands, as unto the Lord.

> For the husband is the head of the wife, even as Christ is the head of the church: and he is the saviour of the body.
>
> Therefore as the church is subject unto Christ, so let the wives be to their own husbands in every thing.
>
> Husbands, love your wives, even as Christ also loved the church, and gave himself for it;
>
> That he might sanctify and cleanse it with the washing of water by the word,
>
> That he might present it to himself a glorious church, not having spot, or wrinkle, or any such thing; but that it should be holy and without blemish.
>
> So ought men to love their wives as their own bodies. He that loveth his wife loveth himself.
>
> For no man ever yet hated his own flesh; but nourisheth and cherisheth it, even as the Lord the church:
>
> For we are members of his body, of his flesh, and of his bones.

A scripture that also supports this is 1 Peter 3:1–7 (NIV).

> Wives, in the same way submit yourselves to your own husbands so that, if any of them do not believe the word, they may be won over without words by the behavior of their wives, when they see the purity and reverence of your lives.

> Your beauty should not come from outward adornment, such as elaborate hairstyles and the wearing of gold jewelry or fine clothes.
>
> Rather, it should be that of your inner self, the unfading beauty of a gentle and quiet spirit, which is of great worth in God's sight.
>
> For this is the way the holy women of the past who put their hope in God used to adorn themselves. They submitted themselves to their own husbands, like Sarah, who obeyed Abraham and called him her lord. You are her daughters if you do what is right and do not give way to fear.
>
> Husbands, in the same way be considerate as you live with your wives, and treat them with respect as the weaker partner and as heirs with you of the gracious gift of life, so that nothing will hinder your prayers.

A woman should keep in mind that this man she is looking for may not initially appear physically as her ideal man. Sure, a physical attraction starts the interest but you may find someone who suits you better that was not catching your eye to begin with. He may not be the chiseled athletic type or the rugged cowboy. This is why you need to rely on God and prayer.

Whether you are a man or a woman, you should be looking at someone and asking yourself, "Will this person be a blessing in my life or a curse? Will we be moving the kingdom forward or will we be seeking counseling later? You should always be looking for the blessing. Not just a blessing that you're not single

THE MAKEUP OF MARRIAGE (ADAM AND EVE)

anymore but the blessing that can move the kingdom forward and have a great family.

It is also important to understand the scripture in Ephesians 5:22, "Wives, submit yourselves unto your own husbands, as unto the Lord," and Ephesians 5:28, "So ought men to love their wives as their own bodies. He that loveth his wife loveth himself." This means the woman stands beside the man and not under him. This scripture does not give men the right to turn their wives into personal servants. Husbands and wives are to work together as one.

LEARNING FROM PROVERBS: MINI SERMON

"Trust in the Lord with all thine heart; and lean not unto thine own understanding. In all thy ways acknowledge him, and he shall direct thy paths."

Proverbs 3:5–6

Let's break this scripture down into parts. Each verse has two parts. So, let us start with the first part of Proverbs 3:5.

The first part says "Trust in the Lord with all thine heart." This means to turn your life over to God. Stop the things that are preventing your blessings. If you lack money, but you still gamble or waste money, God may be saying He cannot trust you with money yet. If you have multiple dating partners, God may be saying he will not bless you with the person of your dreams

LEARNING FROM PROVERBS: MINI SERMON

until you get rid of the sinful nature. Not just get rid of the current dating partners but to get rid of the desire to have multiple partners. Trust your life to God. An example of complete trust would be if God put a blank contract in front of you and said sign it. Would you sign it? Or would you say there is nothing here? Would you demand the contract to be filled out first? Would you want to see the fine print? All of those questions are legitimate questions in the flesh, but we have to trust God, have faith in Him, and not live by sight.

I have talked with several Christian women and they told me they have never dated a saved man. I asked why and they said the pool of men gets too small. This brings us up to the second part of verse 5: "…and lean not unto thine own understanding…" This means that you should not be walking by sight. When we walk by sight alone, we rely on us and what we see. We end up taking the power away from God to help us. The scripture in Mark 6:41–44 says Jesus fed five thousand people with five loaves of bread and two fish.

Could you imagine someone about twenty-five people back in line saying, "There's not enough food. Let's go somewhere and find our own food"? That would have been them living by sight saying there was not enough. They would have missed their blessing, not only for having ample food but to see the miracle by Jesus. We know through God all things are possible. How do we know this, you ask? The scripture says so in Matthew 19:26.

> "But Jesus beheld them, and said unto them, With men this is impossible; but with God all things are possible."
>
> Matthew 19:26

Verse 6 starts with "In all thy ways acknowledge him…" You can start acknowledging God by giving thanks. There is always something to be thankful for. For example, you can be thankful for your health or that you have a job. You could be thankful for your family and kids. We could take being thankful in a different direction and be thankful that your boss does not yell at you like he does the next guy. Or if you are a lady, if you see a man being arrested on the TV, you can be thankful for him not being your husband! Another way to acknowledge Him is to praise Him. Praise God for who He is and for Him being good and truthful all the time. Praise Him for never wavering and glorify Him. The third way to acknowledge Him is by prayer. Pray to God and ask Him to open doors, close other doors; give you the ability to have better discernment, pray for Him to help open your mind to a larger spectrum. Praying and leaning on God means you are putting your life in God's hands. That brings you back to the first part of Proverbs 3:5, does it not?

The second part of verse 6 says "…And he shall direct thy paths." This is God's part of the scripture. We look at the two parts in verse 5 and the first part in verse 6 and see they are intended for man. The last part of verse 6 is God's part. It is a formula that is prescribed by God and we just have to take it. It is kind of like having prescription medication the doctor prescribed you. If you do not take it, you will not get better. God has given us the prescription, you just have to take it.

One of the things my pastor told me was that we need to talk to God more. The more you talk to God, pray to God, glorify God, read God's word, and thank God, the more you will hear from God. This is called delighting yourself in the Lord! This is what we can take out of the scripture Psalm 37:4.

> Delight thyself also in the Lord: and he shall give thee the desires of thine heart.
>
> Psalm 37:4

We delight ourselves in things every day of our life. If we take time to delight ourselves in the Lord, He will see that. God wants to interact with us but we have to start the interaction with God. Let me give you an example from everyday life. If you look at your friends, you will see that some of the characteristics they have you will start to pick up. They start to pick up on some of your characteristics as well. You start to talk alike or phrase things alike or develop the same interests. The more you hang out with someone, the more traits you develop from them. If we take out the words "hang out" and replace it with the word "delight," it would read, "The more you delight yourself in the presence of someone, the more traits you develop from them." This holds true for when we delight ourselves in God. The more we talk to God, pray to God, glorify God, read God's word, and thank God or in other words "delight ourselves in God," the more we find ourselves taking on

God's characteristics. The more we delight ourselves in God, the more we will hear from Him.

Short Review:

- Your most important relationship is between you and God.
- God made a woman from a rib of man to help meet for him.
- Established—companion only or dating for marriage.
- How to talk to and trust God to help you through all of your decisions.
- Don't use the word *but* when hearing from God.
- God blesses sanctified desires.

Now we find someone we like and start to fellowship.

NOTES

FELLOWSHIPPING WITH ONE OR MULTIPLE PEOPLE

Before you start fellowshipping, you should first identify if you are a person who likes to fellowship with only one person or more than one person at a time. This has been an age-old debate as to what is better—to date one person at a time or to date multiple people at a time. It is a topic that I have talked about with many people and I get the same two answers from everyone. It depends on the person. If you are a person who likes to fellowship with multiple people, then you need to find someone who does the same. If you prefer to fellowship with one person at a time, then you need to find someone with those same ideals.

What does not work is when you like to date only one person at a time and the other person wants to date multiple people or vise versa. I have not talked to

FELLOWSHIPPING WITH ONE OR MULTIPLE PEOPLE

one person where there was not an issue of jealousy or awkwardness if they ran into the person on a date. Stay with someone who has the same dating principles.

THE START OF FELLOWSHIPPING

Fellowshipping starts with non-contact fellowship. Yes, I said it, non-contact! This means you do not hug (hold) or kiss for some time. This could be anywhere from several weeks to several months. Hugging good night is acceptable but a handshake will do. I know most people will not like this part but read on for why I say this. The purpose is to understand who the person is. You're getting to know the person and their beliefs. It is called qualifying the person. It's not about romance! What we have to understand is thoughts create words, words create actions, actions create habits, and habits create character. In the beginning, people say and do anything to please the other person. They are on their best behavior. It is called the euphoric phase of the initial fellowshipping/dating. Everyone is on their best behavior, but keep in mind, a lot of people are driven with trying to get sex. Even newly saved Christians still struggle with abstinence. When you take the physical component—sex, cuddling, kissing—away, you will see what they are really like after a short time.

You will find out the answers to questions like do they really like to read the Bible with you, do they really like to pray with you or at all, do they really like to praise God at home or just in church, do they have the desire to move the kingdom forward. Not to mention other everyday things like do they like to have lots of friends around or do they just like to be by themselves, do they really like taking the dog for a walk or do they really like pets at all, do they really like going to the theater for a play or really have an interest in what you like or just in how fast they can charm you into a physical relationship. Plus, you learn what is really important to them. This could range from how much they love tangible things like money, cars, boats, etc., to how important hygiene is to them.

This also gives both people time to get acclimated to being with someone else. If someone has been single for a long time, they will have developed habits as a single person that may need to be changed to incorporate the other person. It may take time for a single person to change or become accustomed to having another person around.

In a secular relationship, once the physical relationship starts, the niceness starts to fall off and the physical becomes the focal point of the relationship. Then a person starts to overlook the negative characteristics and lack in other areas that they normally would not overlook. Some people even put up with abuse, be it physical or verbal or they will put up with demands that they would not put up with if it was just a mutual friend. The sex is what starts to drive them. Everybody desires the physical part but again that is only in the will of God if you are married.

By starting with a non-contact fellowship, you find out if they can keep a job for more than seven days and still be able to keep an objective mind without being clouded by physical contact. Their character should show if they are a provider or a dependent. More so for women, does a man want you to drive all the time or do they want you to pay all the time? Does the man own his own car or does he always get rides? Those are not deal breakers or make the man a bad person, but it should throw up a small red flag. If he does not have a job, a car, his own place, and is constantly relying on other people, you have to realize he is a dependent… dependent…dependent and not a provider. It does not matter how good looking he is, or how charming he is. If you are looking for a provider, this is not the type of man you are looking for. God will provide the person you are looking for, but you may have to be patient and have faith. Again, like I said earlier, those are not deal breakers by themselves and extenuating circumstances can apply. For example, if someone is in school, they may live with a relative, not have a job because they are devoting their time to school and not having a job means no car. The difference in this example is that their vision is for the future. They are going without now so they can better themselves and their family later. So when vision is involved, it can still be a good thing. When there is no vision involved, it is time to move on.

THE START OF FELLOWSHIPPING

This is also the time that the two people would establish visions of their future. The woman should be trying to learn what the vision is of the man and the man should be learning what the vision is of the woman. How do they want to move the kingdom forward? Where do they want their life to go? What do they want to do for a living? Do they want kids? This will be discussed in more detail later in the book.

If your Christian life lines up and you genuinely have the same interests and you have solid ground for dating, then the fellowship can increase to dating, all of which is not clouded by physical attachment caused by kissing, cuddling, sex, etc. When you have established that you are dating, you can open more of your life to them and share more of the hows and whys to move forward in a relationship. Obviously, once you start dating, you can kiss and increase some physical contact as discussed by both parties what is acceptable to each other but still in the will of God.

If during the dating period the man feels like he is growing closer to his rib and the rib feels she is growing closer to her body—being equally yoked—then they can work toward marriage. Then once they are united, it does not stop there. You should always be growing together. If you are not, then you will start to grow apart.

Keep in mind there will be some things men and women will not be able to discuss too much in detail because of our gender. Men will not know or really care about the components of how makeup is applied or made. Men will not know color shades and matching with makeup too. Those topics do not interest men. We just step back and let women do their thing and say, "Just look good!"

The same goes for women too. Most women do not care about what it takes to fix the car or fix the washing machine, they just want it fixed! So, trying to make someone engage in a conversation that absolutely does not interest them is only going to irritate them. These things really are not topics for discussion, they are just kind of understood.

NOTES

HANDLING THE EUPHORIC PHASE

Many people meet someone and immediately think they are falling in love. They find a person that they have been praying for and it appears that this person has all the qualities that they have listed when they were praying. They have the same interests, they get along, they find each other attractive, they dress nice all the time, they have similar plans for the future, they are a good parent (if they have kids); when they text each other, they are using terms of endearment (hun, babe, sweetie), when they speak, everything is all proper and clearly articulated, dinners are well planned, everyone is in good health, etc. This is the euphoric phase of the relationship. Some people call it puppy love, the honey moon phase, or refer to it as being on cloud nine. This is a time where everything is great, and you feel nothing can go wrong; but it's what happens once you get comfortable with the person and some of the persons normal ways of living come out. You will see how some

HANDLING THE EUPHONIC PHASE

characteristics of a person will slightly change. Once the euphoric phase starts to wear off, you will see the person start to dress down and be more casual or even wear comfort clothes a lot more. That it's not always suits, slacks, or jeans, it turns into jogging pants and t-shirt when at home and sometimes when you go out. You will find that some text messages become more direct and skip the terms of endearment and just ask a question or send a reminder. The well-planned dinners that you were used to making at home, become "What do I have in the house that will work?" The "I love you" phrase and reply that was every hour starts to become a couple times a day.

During the euphoric phase, everything seems so great that a lot of characteristics are over looked. No matter what your goals are or your lifestyle or the future you have planned, when you start a relationship there becomes a degree of responsibility. Everything you do as a single person changes. You now have to arrange your schedule with the other persons and incorporate their lifestyle in with yours. You have to be accountable for your time when you're not with the other person so you won't be late when there are plans. You will have to learn someone's living habits, and they will have to learn about your living habits as well.

Regardless of how well your ideals line up for the future and how well you plan and where you see yourself going, you still need to live in the now. You still need to see how the other person lives on a regular basis because the sugarcoating may not always be there. Can you live with the finite changes? Are there habits about the other person that you just can't tolerate? What if while you are in the euphoric phase, you went over to the other person's house for the first time and the house was immaculate. Then over time you came to find out that they leave their cloths all over the house and leave dishes in the sink for a week? Some people live in houses that are just about a sterile environment that you feel could be a model home. Some people like to live in houses that are neat but have that lived-in feel. Their house is not immaculate, but they can live with a little clutter here or there. Some people do not mind clutter at all. Are you someone who takes your shoes off at the door, or do you walk through your house with them on? Would any of these change your impression of them? Would they be a deal breaker for you? For some, it may. Others will say they can deal with that. Others will say they will try to compromise. Each situation is different, and each person is different with what they find tolerable.

Other habits that you will find out after the euphoric phase will be things like sleep patterns, sickness, how they handle frustration. Are they someone who corrects everything to the tenth degree, are they obsessive compulsive with cleaning or scheduling tasks, do they have good hygiene habits, do they act spoiled, do they have any quirks about them that you like or dislike, etc.

These are some of the habits and quirks you will find after the euphoric phase has worn off. Not everyone will experience it, but some will. It's a matter of are you equally yoked enough in the other areas to overcome some of the other quirks and habits of the other person.

HANDLING THE EUPHONIC PHASE

Even if you are equally yoked in many areas, like church, your view on raising kids, your vision for the future, your common interests, you still need to put the other everyday quirks, habits, and ways of living into the picture as well. This is part of your everyday life just as much as your church, your view on raising kids, your vision for the future, and your common interests. These are the little things that make everyday life run for that person. Many overlook these quirks in the beginning and end up becoming a problem in the future. Your everyday actions are what define you, not just your vision and beliefs.

You will also want to spend some time with them to find out if they are a leader or a follower. Do they have standards that they live by, or is anything acceptable? Are they optimistic or pessimistic? Do they take control when something is not going right, or do they add to the chaos?

You may experience someone talking more negatively once the euphoric phase has worn off. You have to ask yourself if the vision for the future is still the same or if it will be tainted by the negative talk. Was the initial dialog between you and them just the happy, puppy love phase, or were they genuine with what they feel? How does someone go from happy, positive, and have a vision of a great future to always complaining or gossiping about others? This would indicate to me that the person's true feelings are coming out after the euphoric phase has ended, and the real evaluation of the person's demeanor and character has to start.

One thing I encourage you to do is to push through the euphoric phase before deciding to get married. In the euphoric phase, everything seems grand and nothing could possibly go wrong. Often it's small quirks or behaviors that a couple has not seen yet in the euphoric phase that gets them. After the phase wears off, they may be thinking *I didn't know he was like this*, or *I didn't know she did that*, both feeling misled. Neither person is misled; they are simply in a hurry to get married. Remember, just because you and your partner attend church and you have a few things in common doesn't mean both of you are meant for marrying each other. You need to push through the euphoric phase to be able to know your partner and be able to trust them.

NOTES

COMMUNICATION

Good communication should not be underestimated. Communication starts from day one. You start to learn about each other, likes, dislikes, habits, and quirks. Talking to each other to learn about each other is the most important thing. You need to know who this person is.

When we talk about the likes of a person, it is easy to hold the conversation especially if you have the same likes as that person. If you are both into the same style of music, then that conversation will never end! The conversation just flows. This is always a great way to start because of your same interest and ability to talk about them and why you like them.

When you get into the dislikes is when the other person's opinion may conflict with your opinion. It could be something as simple as the food they eat. One person may not eat beef or pork and the other person may like everything on the menu. One person might like action movies and the other may not like movies at all. It is important to talk about these things now because if you start to see that your lifestyles do not work, then you can choose to remain friends and move on earlier in the fellowship rather than later. This is not saying if you do not like the same food or the same movies that you should end the relationship. It is merely an example of communicating everything, even the little things. It would be a little red flag that should be noted; too many red flags and you should move on.

Talking about someone's habits is also important. People will have good and bad habits. Good habits that you like about the other person will draw you closer together. It may be something that you did not do before or even think of but you find that you like. The bad habit is an area that can become a focal point in an argument if not addressed early. If you have any issues with someone's habits, put it out on the table early when you start to catch on to them.

Quirks are just little things that make people upset or can also be something that makes them unique. For example, you see someone driving with their blinker on for an extended period of time. Most people do not like that but it drives some people nuts. Little quirks can become big problems when they are added on to something else. The same thing with what makes them unique. Let's say a lady finds a man and realizes he is really into tires. Anytime he hears someone talk about tires he has to put his two cents in and give a complete breakdown on a tire and alternate tires they can buy. This is something that makes the man unique because he is much appreciated in the auto industry however if she has to listen to the tire rundown every day in her relationship it may drive her crazy. Everything else about this man can be great and they can be equally yoked in every other way. She will have to communicate what bothers her about this fascination he has with tires. This is why communication is so important especially talking about the little things. These things may not come up in the beginning of your fellowship, but those little quirks need to be put out on the table so the other person knows it bothers you. How can they stop doing something that bothers you if they do not know that it bothers you? This could be anything from leaving your shoes in the living room to not washing the dishes immediately when done. Some of the quirks you/they may choose to live with because everything else is right in line. You may even find a quirk that you think is cute and says that adds to their personality.

Ultimately, the more you talk the more you learn about each other and the more you can tell the person your likes and dislikes in any category of life. If the dislikes can be worked out and be turned into likes, then fantastic, amen, keep moving forward. It is when you start to see the dislikes are outweighing the likes that you need to put the brakes on and evaluate where the relationship is going. Make a list of things that are not going right or what you think needs to change. This also means talking to the person and seeing what they think too. They may think your relationship is just fine. They may think it is a little rocky but don't know how to address certain issues they have about your relationship. They may be thinking to themselves that they are tolerating the relationship not knowing that you have the same issues with the relationship. They may want the same thing you want but don't know how to address the situation. Again, this is done much easier if you are not having intimate contact with the person.

So, here are two questions that you should ask yourself about your level of communication with your partner:

- How often do you sit down and really talk?
- How much do you know about what your partner does all day?

TEXTING

In today's age, we use texting a lot. Texting is a good form of communication but there should be some cautions to texting.

First things first, get to know the person and their views on texting. Some people are okay with texting but would rather talk on the phone especially if you are making plans to go out. Some people prefer texting over talking. Knowing what the other person's preference is will help the communication lines more.

Second, try to limit jokes or funny punch lines while texting. If it is said verbally, then it may be real funny but the same inflection does not come through on the text. It is not to say do not use any humor at all, just be careful when and how you use it. Just because you put "LOL" doesn't make it funny!

Third, do not panic if someone does not text you back right away, or at all. A couple things apply to this:

1. Did they receive the text?
2. Were they busy or sleeping when they got the text and forgot to text you back?
3. Were they driving and not able to text you back right away?
4. Did their phone get shut off by accident?

Not seeing a response is not always what its seems to be, plus the level of importance you think the text holds may not be the same level of importance the other person holds on it. If it is a very important issue, say that in the text. For example, if you have two tickets on hold and need to know in thirty minutes or less, do not just throw out, "Got 2 tikts 2 the game, do u want 2 go?" What game? What day? What Time? Be specific and let them know there is a time limit. If they do not respond then consider they did not see the text. Now, if the nonresponse continues, you will need to address this in person and let them know that if they receive a text from you, it is common courtesy to text or call back at some point.

Texting can become a hard to understand form of communication when you over-abbreviate. Limit the new abbreviations and stick with common known symbols. I keep using the word communicate. This means communicate and understand what is being communicated. Communication needs to be your strong point in a relationship—that also means understanding text messages. If you do not understand a text message, text back "What does this mean?" or "Call me, I don't understand."

Another thing about texting is texting is impersonal. When you talk, you can hear the inflection in someone's voice and hear how they received what you said. Sometimes, you hear their reaction and the excitement in their voice. You know they received well what you said. Sometimes, if you say something and the person does not receive it well, you can talk to them and elaborate more if they did not understand what or why you said it. In text messages, a person can still not receive what you said well and just discount it by typing "lol. cool, ttyl," but in the meantime they are rolling their eyes saying, "What are you talking about?" then you lose the flow of the conversation. When you talk on the phone, you also hear the person's voice and there is something about hearing someone laugh or giggle at your jokes. There is something to be said about when you say something nice or flattering and you hear the soft *awww*, or just the subtle sounds or softness to their voice that someone can make that you know they are smiling or blushing. There is a connection that is made from the vocal contact.

The last thing I want to bring to light is before you start texting any information about yourself, you should know this: any text or electronic communication—e-mail, Internet, or social media—cannot be taken back once it is sent. It can be forwarded to every phone or throughout the World Wide Web. So a word of caution before you text or do any electronic communication, watch what you send.

COMMUNICATION WHEN YOU DISAGREE

Communication is most important when you disagree because there is tension involved. Anytime you disagree on something, you should first think of finding a resolution to the problem and then work out who was at fault. I understand not all disagreements are that easy to resolve but there is a solution. Anytime you can identify someone being selfish, then the natural solution would be for the person to stop and be more selfless. There are too many topics that can be the cause of the disagreement for me to give examples for each one. My best advice is to try and find a resolution first then talk about who is at fault and how it can be prevented in the future.

A lot of times, our method of working things out comes from how we were brought up. As a child, you learn from your parents and relatives on how to handle certain situations but it goes a little more than just arguing. Your body language tells a lot also. Now, I am Italian and frequently Italians will express themselves by using their hands. Communication with body language should not be overlooked. As you get to know a person, you will see and learn how they communicate, both verbally and physically. This is considered the origin of how we were brought up. Just because you were raised a certain way does not mean you have to stay that way. You may be a person who is saying I was brought up in a household where we raised our voice immediately to get someone's attention. Raising your voice may have a place at some point but not in the beginning. No matter how you were raised, you should want to say, "How can I make myself better to better my family?"

If you are a type of person that holds things in and explodes all of a sudden, then you will find most people will either explode back or try to ignore you because they do not want to hear it. This is a big part of communication, or lack thereof. Disagreements happen. Not everyone sees eye to eye every moment of the day. But it is important that when you disagree on something that you talk it out. Talking allows you to express concern for a particular area but that needs to be addressed and should prompt the other person to talk with you. This is being reasonable. This is responding to the situation on hand and not reacting to it. When you yell and let your emotions get the best of you, things get said that you do not really mean. This then prompts the other person to become aggressive with what they say and they start saying things they do not mean. Inevitably, you get someone taking their words to heart. You may say "I hate you" in the heat of the moment but not mean it. Those words do not solve anything! They only lead to the other person taking you literally. Then later on, when the moment calms down and you feel things should be better, you realize you have a different problem when they say "You said you hated me" then you say "I was mad, I don't hate you", "But you said…" When you find yourself using terms like "Now I know why your ex…" or if you get into name calling, those things only make a situation worse and lends nothing to resolving the issue at hand.

> A hot-tempered person stirs up conflict, but the one who is patient calms a quarrel.
>
> Proverbs 15:18

> Whoever is patient has great understanding, but one who is quick-tempered displays folly.
>
> Proverbs 14:29

Nobody wants to be yelled at and nobody likes to be yelled at. It only adds to the problem. Here's a little side note. One of the antonyms for love is the word *hate*. When you say I hate you, you are not saying, "I'm mad at you." You are saying you no longer have love for them. That may not be what you mean but it is what it gets translated into. That is why you should not speak out of anger but out of concern for fixing a problem.

> Starting a quarrel is like opening a floodgate, so stop before a dispute breaks out.
>
> Anyone who loves to quarrel loves sin; anyone who trusts in high walls invites disaster.
>
> A truly wise person uses few words; a person with understanding is even-tempered.
>
> Proverbs: 17:14, 19, 27

I think it is important to understand that emotions play a big part in how we handle situations. Sometimes, people let emotions take charge of their lives and when something happens, the response is out of that particular emotion and not out of love. When you are mad or bitter at someone and that mad/bitter emotion follows you throughout the day, you will handle the situation out of anger and not out of trying to find the best resolution for the problem. You will say things and not care who gets hurt in the meantime. As a born-again Christian, you will want to take charge of your emotions of being mad, upset, bitter, hurtful, jealous, etc. You have to let the Holy Spirit come out of you and handle your situation. You need to get rid of that negative emotion and yield to the word of God. These negative feelings will always lead you into selfish acts. It is known that emotional people make emotional decisions. Being a born-again Christian, you do not want to put your emotion over the Word of God.

One thing that can be a source of an argument is stress. Stress can come from many different areas like money or lack thereof, difference in opinion, lack of time management, job/employment or lack thereof, living arrangements, etc. Stress is an area that turns a bad situation into a worse situation. Anytime you add stress into your daily life, your regular situations become more complicated. This needs to be identified soon and handled again in a fashion of finding a resolve for the problem, not just wanting to yell. Stress amplifies any problem. If you know you're behind on your rent, there is a small amount of stress involved. If the landlord says he is kicking you out in five days, the stress level goes up. A lot of times, an argument comes about and someone is trying to put fault on who is responsible and the focal point is the problem rather than focusing on the solution. Any time a problem presents itself, you should be trying to find the solution first then discuss the hows and whys. Once you find the solution, go back and discuss how or why the situation happened and then discuss how it can be resolved for the future so it does not happen again.

One thing that needs to be recognized is what the reasoning for the argument is. I have talked with some people and they say they do not argue over pertinent things. Some people get into the knockdown, dragged-out arguments over who is the best singer, who is the best guitar player, why they cancelled a particular TV show, whose French fries are the best, etc. Yeah, I know what you are thinking, do people really argue over that stuff? And the answer is yes! It is very important that you are not letting those kinds of arguments come between you and your partner. You can agree to disagree or present your side and move on. There is no reason to get bound up over who is the best singer. Those are opinionated topics anyway. There are experts in each field and they will pick the top fifty best and still sometimes someone of notable talent does not make the list. Any topic that is based on opinion is not worth arguing over. It is an opinion! Opinions are great when you have the same opinion as the other person. If you do not, then it is okay, it is your opinion. Do not let the devil get into your relationship/marriage like that. Those are unwinnable arguments for both people because they are both right. For the sake of peace in the family, some people find it easier to just concede and say, "You're right, those fries are better," and just move on and not argue, then go buy the fries they like anyways. Others say, "I'm not going to lie," and you will hear their point again and again and again. Like I said earlier, it is an opinion and it is an unwinnable argument. Both people are right because it is their opinion but you should not let it bind your relationship or marriage.

So let us take this into a different direction. This will also be discussed more in detail later in the book. Let us say you have kids in the picture. You could be dating someone with kids or you may have kids yourself. Kids learn from their parents. Every time they see their parents do something, it is like training for them. You see it in every phase of life. If you have overweight parents, there is a good chance the kids are overweight. If the parents are drinkers, the kids start to drink. One of my friends was terrified of storms and as a result their kids were terrified of storms. Same with handling problems—if a child sees their parent handle a situation in a certain way, they think that is how they are supposed to handle it, whether it is right or wrong. If you hold your anger in and you explode, it teaches the kid to do the same thing and not communicate more efficiently. Now, this is not to say that the trend cannot break. There are lots of testimonies that Mom and Dad were heavy and the child stayed thin, or Mom and Dad were bad at holding on to money and just wasted it but the child became very successful. The point is we need to not only be able to communicate to resolve the problem between ourselves but also teach our kids to communicate to handle their problems more effectively too.

One of the best times to address a problem is when it is identified or shortly thereafter. Shortly after is acceptable because the problem may surface when you are out in public where it may not be the most appropriate place to address the problem. Letting a problem hang around will make it worse as time goes on. Addressing a problem when it surfaces is the best time because your matter gets resolved before the issue boils out of control causing an argument on top of the problem.

RED FLAG TO WATCH FOR

One red flag to watch for is what is called question deflecting. Question deflecting is when you ask someone a question and they answer with a question or redirect the conversation in a different direction.

When you have a serious question, you should expect a serious answer. If answers start coming off with a spin or if someone is trying to give you a guilt trip then something is wrong. It is a clear indication of someone trying to hide something. When you ask a question and the answer is in the form of a question like "Why are you asking me that?" followed by "I don't have to justify myself" or "That's just crazy talk," then they are avoiding the question which should prompt even more of an answer.

If a person is trying to give you a guilt trip like saying, "You must be doing something behind my back if you're asking me this," or if they bring up something that you did in the past that has been resolved but just trying to take the focus off of them, then you need to look even more for an answer.

There is another way someone becomes deceiving with their answers and that is by flattery, still in the same context though. If the question requires an honest answer and the person starts with something like a compliment and tries to redirect away from the question there is something wrong as well. Just as an example, when you ask a question and the person says, "Oh, babe, we can talk about that later, you look really hot now!" That line may not come off as smooth as it would in real life but this is a Christian book and I will not use inappropriate language. They are trying to take your focus off the question you asked. Once again, the focus needs to be on the answer to the question not allowing them to take control and redirect the conversation.

What it comes down to is honest questions should receive honest answers. The spin game, guilt game, and flattery game is just that, a game. If you have a serious question, you should expect a serious answer. Anything less and you should start to ask more questions. If the question does not get answered, there should be a bigger red flag. It is not to say time to end the relationship, but it is something that needs to be addressed in the short future. This is where you need to tell the person your concern about communication, and then reflect back on the communication part of this book.

COUPLES WANTING KIDS

Let us take communication in another direction. If you are a couple who has the desire to get married and have kids, you will want to listen to every word of this! As I stated earlier, kids learn from their parents, but it is not always in how to argue. Remember earlier in the book where you read "Thoughts create words, words create actions, actions create habits, and habits create character"? This is primarily true when it comes to raising children. It starts with you fellowshipping and being able to communicate with each other. You need to be able to talk with each other on every level. When something bothers you, you should be able to express that with your partner. Not just in terms of saying "This bothers me" and then turning a blind eye to the problem. The problems need to be discussed and worked out. Turning a blind eye is like putting a Band-Aid on the problem. But since it did not get resolved, the problem will resurface later. As a couple, you not only need to be able to talk things out but to actually work them out. Follow the conversation through. I am telling you this is so important early in your fellowshipping and dating because it is harder to develop later when you are comfortable not talking to each other. Why is it important, you ask? Your kids will see how both of you effectively communicate with each other. In a calm way, discussing the problem, and resolving the problem. What this does for your kids is it will help them feel safe with entrusting their problems to you as a parent! The last thing—let me say this again, the last thing you want as a parent is for your kids to feel like you will be ready to yell or strike them and have them turn to someone else when they have a problem. Let me say that again, you do not want them to turn to someone else! You do not need or want your child going to someone where the first words out of their mouth are contradictory to how you are trying to raise them. Every parent should want their child—no matter what age, 9, 13, 18, and so on—to come to them when they have a problem. Too many times our kids go to other people for advice but they go to the wrong people. They go to their friends who tell them not to tell their parents or they get bad advice on decision making. As a parent, you need to be able to look back and say when you were fellowshipping communication was important because "Words create actions, actions create habits, and habits create character." Our kids learn from us. If communicating is important to us then it will be important to them. Then they will feel safe to come to you with a problem and ask for your advice to help them through their problem instead of going to someone that may mislead them. This also has a secondary factor in it that will bring you closer together as a family because your bond with your kids will be that much stronger. You as a parent will know what is going on in your kid's life and not be estranged to what your kid is doing or how they are growing up.

As a parent, your goal is for the best development of your kids. How you act and treat your kids will be the foundation for how they develop. You are your children's first marriage preparation. What they see is what they will take into their own marriage. You will need to teach them things and teach them in a manner that they will be able to do it themselves. When you give tools to children, it will be with them their whole life. This goes back to the old saying: "Give a man a fish and you will feed a man for a day. Teach a man to fish and you will feed him for life." You are the living role model for your kids. They see your actions and they will learn your values and beliefs. It starts with you!

> Train up a child in the way he should go [and in keeping with his individual gift or bent], and when he is old he will not depart from it.
>
> Proverbs 22:6 (AMP)

It seems some parents may fall into one of two categories: (1) parents that just provide for their kids and the child does not ever learn how to grow up and they just expect someone to do for them, or (2) the parent expects the child to just be able to do it and not teach them anything, resulting in undereducated kids.

You should want to teach your child everything you can so they can be self-sufficient and not have to rely on anyone for basic needs.

Developing your children also entails protecting them at all ages. This means knowing who they are with and having a way of contacting them. Parents will want to make sure their kids are dressing appropriately when they leave to go out to a dance or wherever. Watching what they wear is protecting them from themselves. If a young girl is looking for attention, she will find it more from guys if she is wearing something skimpy. This is why, as a father or stepfather, you need to constantly tell your daughter how beautiful she is and hug her. Letting her know she is loved at home will help prevent her from seeking that attention from another man. When a young lady seeks attention from a man, it usually is a result from her not receiving a certain level of attention at home so she will go elsewhere.

DEVELOPING TRUST

Trust will be one part of the foundation of your relationship and marriage. Trust is not a onetime thing or something that is given to you. It is earned over time. This is why it is good to not rush into marriage until you have developed a level of trust with your partner that you can say you know the person. Trust is developed through experiences. It's not about the duration of time you spend dating. The more things you do to create trust, the faster trust is developed.

Developing trust in your relationship starts from day one. The words you speak and the actions you take will allow someone to trust you more or trust you less. Trust starts with the first plan you make. When you tell a person I will call you at 7:00 p.m. and you call at 7:00 p.m., the person will automatically see you kept your word. If you arrange a fellowship at 6:00 p.m. and you are on time, it shows you are making an effort to keep your word. And just the opposite if you are late calling or showing up. Other things that start the distrust is when you say I will get something done and you do not do it or when you say you will be home at a certain time and get home hours later. When someone sees that you value your word then they can start to value what you say a little easier. Over time, you will develop trust or lack thereof depending on the person you are with and their actions. As you date someone, you will need to develop trust in them for many reasons now and in the future. In the beginning, it is being on time and doing what you said you would do. Later, the questions come up, like "Is this a person that I can trust with my checkbook?" In developing trust, there has to be an effort made. Some people feel they deserve to be trusted without putting forth effort to earn that trust. Trust is earned, not given. Anytime you just give trust, you run the risk of being let down in a big way. Then when someone asks you why you trusted them, you do not really have a good answer. The answers of "They're hot" or "They seemed nice" do not really work too well.

Doing what you say you are going to do in the beginning is very important as well as throughout the relationship. Some people do not realize how easy it is to develop distrust in a person. If you say you will call at 7:00 p.m. and you do not, they will wonder what happened. If that happens several times then the other person will automatically start to write it off like you will not call and eventually say they never call when they say they would. That is a distrust that you don't want. You should value and act on your words accordingly. You want someone to see that you value your words so they can value them too.

One thing you will want to do is keep yourself well-grounded with what is going on in the now. It is okay and important that if someone is doing something that you do not like that you tell them so they have an opportunity to correct it. This would be the right thing to do to develop trust. What you do not want to do is drag the past into the present, especially if the past has been resolved. You do not want to have the mental scorekeeping thing going on. Once you start on the scorekeeping, then it prevents you from addressing the current situation effectively. Anytime you start keeping track, especially over a period of time, it builds stress, it makes the current situation more than what it really is, and interferes with the incident going on right now. Remember, in our relationship, we are developing trust, not keeping score on who did more wrong than right. Once we have communicated something that seems wrong and the other person has corrected their actions, the issue needs to be put into the past and should no longer be an issue. If someone was constantly late and they corrected the problem and started showing up more on time, then the issue of them being late should not come up in an argument later.

It takes time to build trust. It takes time to learn about a person, who they are, what their vision is, what their habits and quirks are as well as if their actions meet their words. This is why communication is so important in your relationship. You should also be mindful of when the other person does make that change in their habit. It should be recognized because then they know you appreciate their efforts.

DEVELOPING TRUST

When you say you can trust me then you are saying you can count on me. This goes for both people. You should be able to identify this pretty easy. You hold the key to someone trusting you. Can they count on you and what you say? Now you have to find out if you can you count on them? Your trust and your dating partner's trust cannot be underestimated. Trust takes time to get, but be careful because it is easy to break, easy to lose, and hard to get back. What you may think is a very minor incident may affect the other person's trust in you and vice versa. If you value your relationship with the other person then you will not want to do anything to break their trust. Above all else you have to trust God where ever He leads you.

BEING EQUALLY YOKED

Being equally yoked is an important part of any relationship/marriage. This means that you agree on a majority of things. What it comes down to is if you are equally yoked, your decision making becomes easier. You know and understand your partner so well that you can almost say what they are going to say. Every decision that has to be made can be made easier because you are both so well aligned. Being equally yoked can range from your common interests to how you view disciplining your kids. It also ranges from decision making to future planning.

Being equally yoked does not have to come in the form of you doing everything the same as the other person. Some circumstances call for the opposite. Two people could be equally yoked if one person loves to talk and the other person loves to listen. They are equally yoked because they are in agreement with each other.

BEING EQUALLY YOKED

Being unequally yoked brings just the opposite. If you both have dominant personalities then both parties have to be right, and if there is a tough decision, then it becomes impossible to make or one party gets very angry after the decision is made.

But let us take the focal point off of decision making. Let us take this into a direction where you are not equally yoked as far as interests. If you have a particular interest in something and your partner does not, it makes it hard to share your accomplishments or even talk to them about that interest. For example, if you are a person who likes to talk about God and what he has done in your life but your partner does not, then you will have some hard times in your relationship because you are unequally yoked.

The same thing with sports. If you play sports or like sports and the other person does not, they may not support your accomplishments or care about any development you have made.

Part of being equally yoked is to understand that you may have flaws and the person you are dating should be your support system. They should be your strength when you are weak and you should be their strength when they are weak. It is what makes marriage run more smoothly. When someone has a downfall, then you can take one of two approaches:

1. Be unsupportive to their weakness, maybe yell or make light of the situation (Not Recommended).
2. You can be supportive of the flaw, keep them lifted up, keep them moving forward, and

just letting them know you care about them (Recommended).

Let me give you an example. If your spouse is a singer but lacks the self-esteem to go up in front of the congregation or anywhere by himself/herself, then you need to be the support system to help him/her through that. You are not supporting the lack of self-esteem by saying there is nothing wrong with not going up on stage, you are saying you will encourage them and help them through this weakness because it will develop him/her more and be able to move the kingdom forward more. If you simply make light of the person and their fear of going on stage or say things that are degrading even if you think you are trying to help, you are still degrading the other person. This does not help the person or move the kingdom forward at all. Let me clarify saying something degrading but thinking you are helping someone. If you say you better get up there or you will never be anything, you are only putting an enormous amount of pressure on the person. Pressure does not help people through their fears—it adds to it. Then if it does not go right, they will have even more of a setback. It is like a coach telling a football player if he does not throw a touchdown on his first try then he will never be a good football player. We all know that would not be true, but that statement might damage his confidence so much because a negative seed was planted. What would be better is if the coach were to encourage the football player to focus more and not let little things bother him. He should not let the little bumps and minor setbacks prevent his progress. A good coach says that was the last play but what we are going to do is this for this play. The coach will encourage him and make it sound as if he has complete confidence in his player to make a great play. Positive thinking results in positive actions. Confidence is nothing more than self-realization. If you take that away from someone then they will not develop. Getting back to the singer, as their support system, you would want to take the small steps too. You would help them by having them sing in front of just you or a small fellowship of people that would also support them. Once the fear is broken on a smaller level, it will help them on the larger level. They need to realize they can do it, and once they do, they will grow in abundance and thank you for supporting them and helping them through their weakness.

If you go the route of yelling, being demeaning, being abrasive with your words, basically the whole motivation-through-fear method, then you are not a good support system for that person. I know being a good support system is just one part of being equally yoked but this is an important part. There has to be a good support system in your relationship.

In the end, both man and woman are looking for their rib or body to form a covenant with each other. As I said before, you do not have to be just like each other to be equally yoked. You have to be in agreement with each other.

PRAYER AND PRAYER FOR EACH OTHER

> And I say unto you, Ask, and it shall be given you; seek, and ye shall find; knock, and it shall be opened unto you. For every one that asketh receiveth; and he that seeketh findeth; and to him that knocketh it shall be opened.
>
> Luke 11:9-10

Here is a short lesson on prayer. First, when you pray, all of your prayers need to be in the will of God. If it is outside the will of God, then God will not manifest it. No ifs, ands, or buts, He will not do it. How do we know if it is in the will of God? God's will is God's word. God's word is the Bible. If the Bible supports it then it is in His will for you.

The second thing you have to have is faith. Without faith, you say you do not believe God can do what you are asking Him for. Hebrews 11:6 confirms this.

PRAYER AND PRAYER FOR EACH OTHER

> "But without faith it is impossible to please him: for he that cometh to God must believe that he is, and that he is a rewarder of them that diligently seek him."
>
> Hebrews 11:6

Now that you know what is in the will of God for you and you have faith that God can manifest it, it is time to pray. Prayer is not about how fancy you can make your words. That does not impress God. Prayer that comes from your heart is what God hears. You do not have to have a two-hour prayer session for God to hear you. Just pray from your heart. The more you pray, the longer you will be able to pray but do not think people just start that way. Another thing about prayer that you want to stay away from is the term "If it's in your will for me." The term *if* is a doubtful word. We know that when the Bible says it, it is in God's will for us. You need to be specific in your prayer. Saying you want a husband or a wife is too general. How will God give you His best if you do not know what you want for yourself? An idea before you pray for a new husband or wife is to make a list of qualities that you want to see in them. The list could be a variety of things such as pleasant to the eye, works well with kids, wants kids of their own, wants to move the kingdom forward. Your list will be different from everyone else's list because you know the type of person you like. You can also list traits that you do not want to see in the person either, like a person who would be rude, arrogant, condescending, unreliable, and pessimistic. God hears your prayers the first time. Your prayers after the first time are just a reminder that you are still holding God to His word. This is where faith comes in. Some people want that instant faith. They pray and God gives right then. God does do that but not in every situation. Sometimes God will want to see where your level of faith is. Is your faith time limited or is it indefinite? If you pray for a wife or husband and they do not manifest in a month, will you say that is what you thought and give up or will you say they are on their way? Sometimes, God will make you test the prolonged faith to make sure you are being true. But the reward on the other side is that of a greater magnitude that you may not even think of. You may be praying for a wife and have a certain expectation, but God will bless you with someone far more than what you dreamed of. You might be praying for a husband and God will give you a provider for more than what you could imagine. Remember what the scripture says about man and God. When we rely on us to get a spouse, we are limited; but when we rely on God, all things are possible.

> But Jesus beheld them, and said unto them, With men this is impossible; but with God all things are possible.
>
> Matthew 19:26

Notice the scripture says, "All things are possible." Not *some* things or *most* things, but *all* things. Sometimes, we as humans put limitations on God and think that he is limited to earthly or human standards and abilities. If you pray and stay faithful, God will manifest it for you. Remember, it must be in the will of God. One thing that is not in the will of God is divorce. So if you know of someone who is in a bad marriage and you feel you could be a better husband/wife for that person, praying for a divorce is not in the will of God! If the divorce happens, that will happen in God's time. As a Christian, you should be praying for the divorce not to happen. I know if my marriage was having troubles, I would want people praying for my marriage to get better, not praying for a divorce where someone else wants to be with my spouse. Wouldn't you agree?

Prayer is important in every relationship. Developing a good prayer life makes for one piece of the relationship. It is important to listen to your partner when they say they need prayer. This does not mean pray for me when you get home. It means I want some prayer now! Even if one says pray for me when you get home, that is all good and you can pray when you get home but the matter exists now so why not pray now. Praying for each other now is not just in time of need, it is also praying for the future. What you sow now you will reap a harvest from later.

Remember when you pray try to use scripture. This is God's word and God's word is always true. If your prayer is supported by scripture then it is in God's will for you.

Taking relationships, for example, if you are a man and desire to get married, the scripture says in Genesis 2:18, "It is not good for man to be alone." This shows that if the man should want a wife, there will be one for him. Sometimes it may not happen right away, but it will happen through prayer and faith.

I think most people would agree that when you find someone to fellowship with, you would like to know sooner rather than later if the person is right for you. It is a part of not wanting to waste time. You want to know if the person you are talking to is being upfront with all they are saying or is it a mask to cover up who they really are just to lure you into a physical relationship. Some people will say they are Christian and be nice, but you will want to learn if they are genuinely honest about what they are saying or if it is a cover to get close to you. Some of the things you do to qualify the other person is to look at who influenced them. Do they have a giving nature or a taking/selfish nature? It is known that people with good character surround themselves with good positive people and have a positive attitude. This also means you want to look at what is important to them. What do they do verses what they say.

This is why it is important that as you enter into fellowshipping, you need to rely on God. Sometimes, things seem too good to be true and they are. It is a trick by the devil to take you off the right path of finding the right person for you. Sometimes, they are the real thing and God is saying this is the person I have blessed you with. The difference is, are you trying to listen to God, or are you taking the flesh and running with it? Do you listen to the warning signs, or do you ignore the warning signs?

> "But when you ask him, be sure that your faith is in God alone. Do not waver, for a person with divided loyalty is as unsettled as a wave of the sea that is blown and tossed by the wind."
>
> James 1:6 (NLT)

Say a prayer: Lord, I come to you in the name of Jesus. I know I can only lean on you to help me. Please give me a fast discernment on this fellowship. That if this person is not my rib or body then let that become prevalent rapidly. Let the cause of the deception be unveiled so I can move forward with finding the true person for me so we can move the kingdom forward together. In Jesus's name, amen!

Prayer is also important for raising your kids as well. As a parent, you are covering your kids through prayer. When your kids go through something spiritual or sickness, it is up to you as the parent to pray for them and teach them to do so for when they grow up. When your children are young, they will not be able to identify spiritual attacks or know as much about prayer and faith as an adult. This is why you cover your kids and teach them at the same time. They learn from your actions and see your habits. This will become a part of them that they will pass on in their family as well.

Some people have a hard time praying out loud. There could be several reasons, they may be afraid of making a mistake in articulating their prayer, they may have anxiety when they are around someone who is really good at praying, they may feel embarrassed of how they pray, but whatever the reason is, start with short prayers and let them develop. If you are a person who has a hard time praying out loud then let your partner know and start slowly and build on your prayers. Prayer books are a good way to help articulate your thoughts, however use them in addition to your prayer. God wants to hear it come from your heart, not come from your memory alone. You don't have to be perfect, just have the desire to get better.

I would like to take a moment to talk about keeping focused on prayer itself and identifying patterns or rituals. God is not an admirer of rituals or customs. You need to believe in God and His ability more than what you do, where you do it, when you do it, and how much you do it. God does not care if you go in the same room and pray at the same time and drink the same drink before or after your prayer session. Remember, in James 1:6 where it says, "Be sure that your faith is in God alone." It does not say have faith in God and the manmade rituals you practice. Like I said earlier, God does not care if you are in the living room or dining room. Walking around the couch seven times does not impress God and make Him hear you more. God hears repentance, thankfulness, praise, worship, and hears you when you have prayer for sanctified desires.

If you are not seeing your prayers being answered then there may be something else going on. Here are five steps to help you receive the prayers you have been asking for:

- Your prayers must be in the will of God. 1 John 5:14–15
- Humble yourself before God. James 4:6

- Turn away from any reoccurring sinful nature. James 4:7–8
- Pray with all your heart. Jeremiah 29:13-14
- Pray to understand God's will and for His glory. Colossians 1:9

ESTABLISHING VISION

Dating is also the time that the two people would establish visions of their future. It is important to remember that God gives man vision and the vision is more than what is going on right now. The vision is always what can be. The woman should be trying to learn what the vision is of the man and the man should be learning what the vision is of the woman. First, it is nice to find someone that has a vision. Without a vision, you are going nowhere! But let us say you are fellowshipping with someone and they appear to have solid Christian values and the way they move the kingdom forward lines up with how you like to move the kingdom forward. One part of the vision is moving the kingdom forward. You still need to learn more about each other's vision. Do both people want to get married at some point? It is not a proposal but needs to be established relatively soon because if one person has a desire to get married and the other does not, then they need to remain friends and not lead one person on. The person who wants to get married will just be wasting time trying to convince the other person and it will inevitably end poorly for the one who wants to get married. Do both people want kids? Same idea. If one wants kids and the other does not, the fellowship should not escalate to dating. Everything else may be great but if a pregnancy happens (once married), then someone will be bitter and it will cause a strain in the marriage and that may lead to divorce. Remember, we are trying to pair up with our rib or our body, not trying to make a poor relationship work. It is like putting a square block into a round hole. If you hit it hard enough, you can eventually jam it through, but that does not mean it was meant to fit. Obviously, there will be things that do not line up perfectly in a relationship and that could be based on gender, age, habits, or particular tastes.

So let us say your Christian walk lines up, both want to get married at some point, both want kids or not, you still have to look further into the vision. Let us say one's vision is to take them in one direction and the other person's vision takes them into another direction. Are they still compatible? For example, a man is in a band and the band travels. The lady's vision is to own her own business and she will also travel or even relocate. Can they work the travel or relocation out or do they opt to not escalate the fellowship to dating? Remember, you are prequalifying the other person before you start dating. Remember also that it is better not to marry at all than to marry the wrong person if there are signs that it will not work out, therefore, ending in divorce.

As you establish vision, you are planning for the future. How are you planning on living? How are you going to raise kids, if you have any? The simple things that gets overlooked, like who pays the bills, cooks dinner, takes care of the pets, takes the kids to practice, and so on. This is all in your vision or the planning phase. The old saying goes "People don't plan to fail, they fail to plan!" Life is not something that we want to fail to plan in.

You will also want to establish finances as well. How will you save, how much will you save, what will you be willing to save for (college, new car, new house, kids future marriage), will you plan on leaving an inheritance, etc.? The Bible shows in Proverbs that God wants us to leave an inheritance for our children's children.

> A good person leaves an inheritance for their children's children, but a sinner's wealth is stored up for the righteous.
>
> Proverbs 13:22

Let us take vision in a different direction. Everything that we have talked about is us preparing for the future. One thing that happens to us is when a problem hits us and we lose our vision for the future. We deal so much with the *right now* and, to some degree, rightfully so, but as a person with good vision, they do not let a problem take them away from their vision. It is like building a building to put your new business in. When you start building and a contractor says it will be delayed, your vision should not stop for owning your own business, even if the building takes much longer to build than normal. You do not, or should not, lose your vision of having a business, right? When something comes up, it is important to look beyond the problem so you can see yourself getting past your problem. Some people get a problem and let it stick with them even long after it is resolved. They deal in the "remember whens" and "I should haves" but cannot see past the initial problem. They feel they should be so much further ahead. They feel like I should have been making money now and I would have been able to do this or that. They cannot get away from the delay as opposed to those who say this is not going to stop me. The people with good vision and faith know they have not been denied but only delayed.

Let us say your vision is taking you and your family to a new house and new location and you get laid off. Some people dwell on the fact of where they would have been if they did not get laid off but are not doing anything to get back on track. How do you handle adversity? Do you let the layoff derail you or do you say you are going to find a way to keep your vision? Finding a way shows a strong character and faith in God. Sitting back complaining how you got the short end of the stick just shows lack of faith in God and poor character.

DATING TIPS AND GUIDELINES FOR SAFETY

Here are some dating guidelines that should be used for safety and keeping the fellowship moving smooth. I have mentioned some things in these guidelines that may seem like non-Christian traits or habits, but, again, these guidelines are designed to keep someone safe. It is my intent to do so for everyone. There may be new converts or someone who just cannot shake a particular part of their life just yet and we will have something in here for them.

As you plan your fellowship, plan something that you can talk with the person during the fellowship. Going to a movie may be fun but you do not talk. Make plans to do something where you can interact with each other.

Fellowshipping with someone for the first time can begin several different ways. First, how do you know the person? Are you friends with them or were you just introduced? Have you known them as a friend for a long time or just an acquaintance? These questions will reflect how your first fellowship goes and what level you are at. If you have known the person for a long time and have been friends with them, this will give you a little more security in them and how they will treat you and respect you, plus you should know a little more about their views on God. This also opens up the first fellowship to a larger spectrum of things to do than if you just met the person and need to develop trust with the person.

When you fellowship someone for the first time that you have just met, meet during the day in a public place like a restaurant, or wherever there is a crowd. Do group activities like double dating, or if there is no group, then do something like play miniature golf. Some other fun activities you can do if they are available to you are going to the zoo or going to a nature conservatory like the one in Niagara Falls (or one close to your area), but choose places that have lots of people present. If the two of you are alone and not with a group, then have lunch, not dinner (if possible). That way, you will build in a time limit. Building in a time limit is good because it is easier to say goodbye without any peer pressure at 5:00 p.m. than it is at 11:00 p.m. At 5:00 p.m., you have the ability to end the fellowship for the evening, letting the person know you have other things to do. It could be anything from studying to doing laundry. The point is, at 11:00 p.m., most people do not start studying or doing their laundry. They are winding down to go to work the next day. It is harder to tell a person you want to end the fellowship for that night if they are pressuring you to spend just a few more minutes together. Doing something in the daytime not only gives you an early end time but it also allows you to extend the evening if things are going well and you both want to continue to talk. This gives the best time allowed because you do not have to sacrifice sleep to get to know someone.

Things you want to stay away from on first fellowships or in the early beginnings is anything that requires a lot of work or skill. For example, some people may find hiking fun, but if one person does not find it as fun as you do it makes for a long day. Not to mention you will be very tired. You want to end your day feeling good about how it went, not how wiped out you are. The same with playing a sport like tennis. If the other person is not coordinated, it makes for a frustrating day, not a day of learning about each other. This time in the beginning is time you spend to get to know the person. Definitely do not go to secluded places by yourself. (This means boat rides, campgrounds, parks, a friend's house, etc.)

If you have known the person for some time and have been friends with them, your first fellowship can open up a few more options. This would lead you to believe that you know some of the other person's interests/ beliefs and have a larger selection of things to choose from like going to a comedy club or improv

DATING TIPS AND GUIDELINES FOR SAFETY

show, aquarium, art museum or gallery, playing billiards, eating at a restaurant with great food and a fun atmosphere, bowling, seeing some live music at a small venue, going to a sporting event, cooking out in the park, going to a botanical garden, going to a fair, getting ice cream, feeding ducks, going to the pond to feed the - in place of feeding or even in wintertime around the holidays, you can go for a Christmas light tour. While on some of these ideas you may not be able to have constant conversation, you will still have something to talk about a long time afterwards to reflect back on. These are acceptable fellowships since you have already known this person for some time so the initial getting-to-know-the-person is already done.

As a safety tip for a first date/fellowship, it is a good idea to let a friend know who you are going with, where you are going, and about what time you should be done, especially if you are in college. Let someone know your location and how long you plan on being there, when you are leaving, your route home, etc., to establish a timeline.

Until you really get to know the person, have your own transportation and have your own money. Carry enough money for your own meals, tickets, and so on. Do not depend on anyone financially. It is okay to let someone pick up the check but not if it comes with a price. This goes for both men and women. If at any time during your fellowship you feel the time spent together is not going well, you know you have a definitive end time. When dinner is over, you say goodnight and the fellowship is over. Having your own transportation and money allows you to leave much easier than to have to further that night with driving them home and risking awkward conversation. I try not to give too many of my life examples in this book, but before I adopted this rule, I had one time where I wished the date could have ended right at the end of dinner because of her actions. I knew the ride to her house was going to be miserable because she had a few drinks. When we were just talking, she said she only drank casually but not to get drunk. What I did not realize was a few drinks made her lose her ability to have a regular conversation and turned her into an arguing machine over anything, and as a result, it took me forty minutes to get her out of my car once we got to her house. This brings me to my next point—do not use drugs or alcohol.

I understand what the Bible says about not drinking until drunkenness. I am not contesting that scripture; however, I strongly encourage everyone not to do anything that impairs or alters your mind. As Christians, we should be trying to make our body better, not giving reason for someone to take advantage of it.

I strongly encourage you to not drink. However, if you do drink, know your limits. When you drink, the first thing you lose is your judgment. Even without drinking, Christians have a difficult time handling temptation, not to mention if the temptation is greater on the other person's part than on your part. You do not want to put yourself in a dangerous situation of being attacked.

COLLEGE STUDENTS

College students often do not have cars or are in areas that they can walk to meet their date at. Here are some more tips if you are a college student having to walk back to your dorm.

There are some steps you will want to take when you are on campus. A great deal of college crime unfortunately takes place at night and involves people who are walking on campus. Walk with another person or a group of people. Walking with another person greatly reduces the chance that you will have some sort of problem or face some sort of campus crime. If you do end up walking alone, there are some important practices that you will want to incorporate into your routine:

- Take care to stay in well-lit areas
- Pay attention to your surroundings
- Try to walk close to populated areas
- Call someone before you leave and let them know your route and estimated time of arrival
- Know emergency phones locations across the campus
- Check with campus security to compare each campus and see if there is any different information about that particular campus
- Check with campus police to find out if there are any areas that are more problematic than others, to establish better routes back to your dorm

- And, finally, keep the campus security phone number handy. That means program it into your cell phone. Do not hesitate to call campus security if you need a ride from one point to another at night. It always is best to be safe rather than become the unfortunate victim of a campus crime.

It is important to remember that colleges and universities are generally safe places. Students are usually safer, statistically, on their college campus than they are off campus. Because campuses are safer, it can lead to students often letting down their guard. Therefore, the bottom line is that there is no substitute for personal vigilance when it comes to campus safety.

An important part in seeking God when you are fellowshipping is to give thanks to God after every fellowship and ask for guidance and discernment. God wants to guide us. You just need to receive what He is telling you.

NOTES

TOPICS OF DISCUSSION

QUESTIONS TO HELP UNDERSTAND YOUR POTENTIAL DATING PARTNER

This section is to help facilitate getting to know someone. These questions in "The Heart of the Matter Questions" are designed for you to get to know the person and to be able to determine earlier in the fellowship if you are somewhat compatible. You will want to see if any of these questions are drawing red flags, especially the church questions. Remember, if the person is not saved and they do not go to church, they will not have the same connection with God that you do. It is not your job to date someone and bring them to the Lord. You do want to bring people to the Lord, but if they choose not to follow, you will probably end up hurt emotionally. If you like them, bring them to the Lord first then increase your relationship. If they like you, then they will see how good the Lord is and the goodness the Lord can bring them. If they do not want to see the light, you cannot make them, and it is time to move on.

When you are talking to someone, your conversations should flow. If you are finding it difficult to talk to the person, let them know. Let them know what is making you uncomfortable, or ask if there is a reason why they are uncomfortable. Sometimes, breaking the ice like that helps free the conversation up.

With these questions, answer them as honestly as possible. Sometimes, you may have a way of dealing with a situation or may not have a good way of dealing with a situation that the other person can help you with. For example, the question, How do you respond to someone who asks you out when you are in a relationship? They may not have a good way of turning someone away, they may choose to avoid the person after that. I would answer that question with a simple respectful decline. I would tell them I am flattered they think of me like that, but I am in a relationship and I love the person very much, and would not do anything to jeopardize it. I would wish them the best and not treat them any different than before. Keep in mind, if someone has an interest in you, regardless if you are dating someone or not, you should be flattered even if that person is not your type but there is no need to be rude or evade someone if they have an interest. Just be polite and move on. They will respect you more for your honesty then the cool spin (lie) you can give them.

This section is also designed to see how well you are aligned with someone else's thinking. It's designed to see if you think alike. Many times, people avoid certain topics that they might have a conflict in and that does nothing to help learn about a person. When you discuss topics, you will see if the person is optimistic or pessimistic. You will see if they share the same views as you or if your views conflict. You will share views, opinions, and life stories that the other person can associate with and even learn from or you will find the disagreement in what you talk about. This is a time to be honest about you and not try to give answers thinking it is what they want to hear.

This section is divided into four parts, the Heart of the Matter Questions, General Conversation Questions, Fun Conversation, and Questions for Later. Certainly ask whatever questions you feel are appropriate. You are not limited to just these questions. These are to get the ball rolling and identify qualities of someone quickly.

This section is not intended for you to take the book and sit down in front of the other person to read as if you were conducting an investigation. Pick some questions to talk about and let your conversations flow. There is no particular order to ask these questions. You will see that sometimes people will offer up information about themselves even without asking a question. This is also why it is important to listen. If someone tells you something and you are not paying attention, then asking the question will show you were not listening.

You know, like when someone says they have two kids and how they love both kids so much then a few minutes later you come up with what you think is a good question of how many kids do you have? It just shows them you weren't listening.

Listening also tells the other person, "I want to learn more about what you think and feel." It is letting them know what they say is important to you. In James 1:19, the scripture reads "My dear brothers and sisters, take note of this: Everyone should be quick to listen, slow to speak ..." NIV

Even if you're not a conversationalist, just by listening to what someone is saying will help you develop questions to ask about them.

THE HEART OF THE MATTER QUESTIONS

1. Are you currently in a relationship?
2. Do you go to church?
3. Are you saved?
4. What church do you attend and how often?
5. Are you in any church ministries?
6. Who has been your biggest influence in your life?
7. How is your relationship with your parents?
8. Where do you work?
9. How long have you worked there?
10. What are your goals in the near future?
11. What are your future long-term goals?
12. Who are the people you depend on?
13. Who are the people that depend on you?

14. Who are the people you think have made a difference in your life?
15. Do you want to get married someday?
16. Have you ever been married?
17. Do you want to have kids?
18. Do you already have kids?
19. If you are dating someone whose denomination is different, what denomination will your child be raised under?
20. When do you take time to pray?
21. Since God wants us to be forgiving, how have you handled a situation where someone has wronged you?
22. Should parents monitor their kid's mail/e-mail/social networks?
23. Can you live with someone who has different political views than you?
24. How do you respond to someone who asks you out when you are in a relationship?
25. What three things are most important to you in a relationship?

GENERAL CONVERSATION QUESTIONS

1. Where did you grow up?
2. Do you have any brothers or sisters?
3. Where did you go to high school?
4. Where did you go to college?
5. If you could do it again, what career/life choices would you do different?

TOPICS OF DISCUSSION

6. What is your favorite television program, movie, CD, book, and/or website?
7. How do you spend your days off?
8. What is one of your worst fears?
9. What is one of your favorite Bible verses and/or stories?
10. How do you handle your money? Are you a spender or a saver?
11. Do you look at price tags when you shop or do you just get what you want and not worry about the price or getting a deal?
12. If you could afford any car, which one would your buy?
13. When you do not feel good, what makes you feel better?
14. Would you call the family you grew up in a religious family? Why or why not?
15. What do you think of the phrase "If you can't say something good about someone, don't say anything at all"?
16. What has been your most life-altering event?
17. Have you ever done something that was wrong knowing it was wrong? How did it make you feel?
18. What was one of your favorite subjects in school?
19. Who do you get along with better, your mom or dad? Why?
20. If you could change anything in the world, what would you change?
21. Name one time when someone helped you more than they will ever know?

22. Do you like to travel?
23. If there were any place in the world you could travel to with an unlimited expense account, where would you go? Why?
24. If you could spend three, six, twelve months with anyone, dead or alive, who would it be?
25. Same question, but give an answer different from Jesus this time?
26. What is your favorite way to spend an evening during your workweek?
27. Is nutrition important to you?
28. How would you describe the perfect house, including the décor, furnishings, appliances, and landscaping?
29. Is punctuality important to you or is it okay to be a little late?
30. Do you like everything to be well planned and organized or are you more casual and spur of the moment?
31. Can you talk openly about everything?
32. Does age matter in a relationship?
33. Who is your favorite gospel artist?
34. Why do you think people fast?
35. Some youth leagues give trophies to every child, win or lose. What is your opinion on that? Should only the winner get trophies and push the others to try harder or should everyone get a trophy so their feelings do not get hurt?
36. Do you like sports? If so, what sport(s)?
37. What do you like about your favorite sport?
38. What sport do you like the least? Why?

39. Is losing associated with being a loser?
40. What do you like to spend money on when you recreationally spend money?

FUN CONVERSATION

1. Talk about when you or your family helped a neighbor, friend, or stranger, and how it affected them and you.
2. Talk about something humorous that happened at church.
3. Talk about your favorite comedian and why you like them.
4. Describe one of your favorite family celebrations, if any. If none, what would you like to celebrate on an annual basis?
5. Name some things that annoy you. Why do they annoy you?
6. What is one of your earliest memories of God?
7. Give one testimony of how God has worked in your life.
8. Give an example of a prayer that you felt was answered.
9. If you could live anywhere in the world, where would it be?
10. Describe your perfect holiday?
11. What is your favorite animal?
12. What is your favorite type of Food (Italian, French, etc.)?
13. What would be your favorite dinner? (Include everything from appetizers to dessert.)

14. Give an example of a prayer you felt was not answered. Does the Bible support that prayer? How did you handle that?
15. What would you consider a perfect date? (Give examples for different times of the year.)

OTHER QUESTIONS FOR LATER

Originally, I was not going to address any questions, but one question that kept coming up was how will we make decisions when we disagree? I can only give some insight to this and a suggestion. First, you have to recognize that when a decision needs to be made and there is a disagreement, 99 percent of the time, the person who wins that battle is the person who is more passionate about their decision. Keep in mind, the more passionate person may not always be right. Even the smallest voice will be heard if there is enough passion to it.

When it comes to disagreements, I look at the problem first because every problem is different. For example, if a husband and wife are looking at purchasing a used car and there are two they can choose from, both cars are the same cost, both cars support their needs, but they differ in other areas—one car may get 47 miles to the gallon and the other gets 16. The car that gets 16 mpg is the color one person wants and has a great stereo system, but the other car has little features.

In this instance, the decision has to be based on operational needs, a practical use for the family, and a vision for what will happen in the future. If you buy the car that is the color that you want and has a great stereo but gets 16 mpg, in a month's time, the stereo and color will not matter, but what will matter is when you are at the gas pump having to fill your tank three times as much.

The decision making should not be based on wanting the other person to be happy that they got what they wanted because at some point they may realize what they wanted was not the best choice and then they will fault you for letting them make that decision.

When it comes to making these types of decisions, the decision has to be made in the best interest of the family. If you can identify any selfishness in your decision making, then it does not work for the good of the family. Your selfishness is just turning to foolishness.

I brought this up because I had a friend who wanted a real expensive BMW. He wanted to save money on the side but not tell his wife, then one day just show up and tell her he bought it. Now, they had all kinds of financial debt, car troubles, child support issues, and here he was thinking about buying an expensive car. Does this seem selfish or for the good of the family?

So below, I have a list of questions that should be taken seriously. These are questions that will be keeping areas of you marriage straight, aside from just how well you get along with the person. If you are asking these questions, then you are probably considering getting married.

1. How will we budget?
2. Will we have separate accounts and handle separate bills?

3. Will we have a joint account for house bills and our own account for recreational spending?
4. Who will do the record keeping?
5. How will we make financial decisions together?
6. How will we make decisions when we disagree?
7. Who will do the cleaning?
8. Who will do the cooking?
9. Who will do the laundry?
10. Who will do the grocery shopping?
11. Are you willing to negotiate household chores?
12. Are you willing to take premarriage counseling with me?
13. Is there anything about your past that I do not know but should be aware of?
14. If you could change one thing—anything!—about me, what would it be?
15. What are you not willing to give up for our marriage?
16. Can you identify inner fears about our future relationship?

NOTES

DATING WITH CHILDREN

A good idea if you have children and are looking to date is to not introduce your children to the other person right away. This should only be done if you have determined that you can be serious in your relationship with the other person.

One thing any Christian parent does not want to do is introduce a potential dating partner to their children right away for several reasons:

- First, you may not know this person too well, and if the fellowship does not work out early then you do not want your kids seeing you constantly bring in new potential dating partners. Remember you are your children's first influence of how to act. If they see you fellowshipping with different people on a regular basis, they will feel that is what they

- should do too. They may not realize your fellowship just didn't work out.
- Second, you should not introduce your kids to anyone that you are not sure of because you do not want them to develop attachments to the person in case you determine the fellowship is not going to turn into anything more.
- Third is a safety issue! If you do not know the person, you will not know their intentions, motivations, habits, or quirks. The last thing you want is for your child to start to like someone that has a very different view from you on any notable subject. You would hate to think that you are dating a standup person but then they turn out and say something that totally contradicts what you are teaching your child.

I remember once a girl was trying to tell me how Christian she was and that she was saved. She said she was very giving and always had the best intentions for her kids. But when I asked her if she attends church on a regular basis, she said no, she doesn't attend church at all. She felt that all pastors were corrupt and did not feel she could be lead spiritually by a corrupt person. I do not know where she got that idea from or her life experiences, but I do know that if I had kids, I would not want her telling my kids this. Now, we were not dating or even trying to date but I was using this as an example of why it is important not to bring just anyone around until you know more about them and where they are in their walk with Christ.

You also want to find someone who likes your kids number one. They need to like your kids so they can love your kids when you are married. Your kids need to like the person too. If they do not like each other, then you will find a tough marriage ahead of you. You cannot force your kids to like anyone but they should like a quality person. Keep this in mind. If you see the word *selfish* in your decision making, then you are not making a decision for your kids or family. Once you have kids, you need to put them first. Their development is the most important part right now. How hot the guy or girl is does not even reach the same playing field. A hot guy or girl but negative atmosphere does not help in your child's development one bit. It only takes away from it.

Let me clarify being selfish. Being selfish is putting your flesh desires first, not thinking how it will affect your kids. You should be trying to find the right person for you and your kids. This is where vision comes in. When your kids grow up and move out, how will you be with your spouse? Your relationship with your dating partner and future spouse has to be the most important next to your relationship with God. Your dating partner has to be on the same page with raising your kids as you are. Raising your kids is so important for the future generations. Your kids will be the one moving the kingdom forward and working the jobs moving our workforce forward. Again I go back to your relationship with your dating partner. Once the kids move out, how good is your relationship? You don't want your relationship with your spouse centering around your kids because it may dissolve when the kids move out.

NOTES

INTERRACIAL DATING

A question was asked to me: "Is interracial dating biblical?" Let's just start by saying there is nothing in the Bible that says it is non-biblical.

I was having a discussion with a contractor that was building my garage, and he said interracial dating wasn't biblical. I asked where he saw that at because I never read that in my Bible. He said it was in 2 Corinthians chapter six. In 2 Corinthians 6:14, Paul says, "Do not be yoked together with unbelievers. For what do righteousness and wickedness have in common? Or what fellowship can light have with darkness?" This only discusses the idea that believers should not be dating or married to unbelievers. What it comes down to is God loves us all. God created us all, and that includes the color of our skin. We are of a Christian race.

Let us go back to the part of being told to read our Bible. In Genesis, we learned that God created all things, including Adam and Eve. Adam and Eve gave birth to all the nations. In the New Testament, Jesus breaks down that there are no differences between Jew or Gentile, just believers and non-believers. So when it comes to interracial dating, you are able to date and be biblically sound. While culture may be more prohibitive of interracial dating and marriage, God accepts all people no matter who they are. God's word tells us that dating should be based more on beliefs than on race, and that people need to be equally yoked to one another rather than share an ethnicity or skin color.

Some people let culture dictate who they date, or they let a friend or someone else talk them out of dating a good person not in their race. You cannot let someone's opinion of race or skin color affect your decision of dating someone from another race. Anyone who tries to belittle you, tell you they are disappointed in you, or try to make you feel guilty or bad for dating out of your race is only trying to hold you back because of their own beliefs. They are trying to draw on your emotions and your friendship with them, like what you are doing is wrong. Why would you listen to this? Their opinion is based on skin color and ethnic origin, nothing biblical.

Let us take the same views on another subject. What if they try to belittle you, tell you they are disappointed in you, or try to make you feel guilty or bad for being a Christian? It would probably upset you if they said they cannot believe you would be going to church and giving your money to people and you do not even know where it goes, that you are a loser now and expected more from you? They are attacking your beliefs. They are people you would not want to be around. So if you listen to anyone say this about someone you are trying to date then you are living a life out of someone else's expectations and not your own. Do you think the person you like and feel God has given you is not good enough because your friend (or whoever) does not like their race or skin color?

So my question is "Why would you let someone else's opinion affect your decision on dating a great person?" Can you consider them a friend? Are you listening to someone who does not want to see you happy? Are they just hating because they do not have the same thing? The longer you listen to them, the longer it will take you to find true happiness with the one God has in mind for you. You have to recognize that this is the work of the devil and let the Holy Spirit bubble up inside of you and let out a little laugh when you recognize it. It is so much easier to handle the nonsense when you let God take over. Remember the scripture, cast your cares because He loves you.

> "Casting all your care upon him; for he careth for you."
>
> 1 Peter 5:7

Dating someone outside your race for the first time may be different for you at first because of fear of the unknown. The fear of the unknown is what prevents some people from taking the step into interracial dating. Every culture and every family has a history. Some families have particular things they like to do on a regular basis or different times of the year. You will not know everything about the other person or their culture and vice versa. This is a time to share your life with them. Introduce them to your favorite foods, movies, books/authors. Sometimes, there are even cultural festivals that come around. Those are great for giving some insight into ethnic culture and what makes it special. Understanding different parts of another culture will help you through the beginnings of dating. Some cultures use a strong handshake as a sign of confidence; others show a limp handshake as a sign of warmth and possibly sexual attraction. Other cultures will kiss you on the cheek when they greet you while some will bow to you instead of shaking your hand. The more you learn about each other and the culture surrounding both of you, the more you can understand how race/culture will affect both of you. The benefit to this is you can connect on a deeper level. It is called life enrichment. The more you do this, the more you understand the person and the culture they came from. This also helps prevent cultural misunderstandings. Keep an open mind to trying new things that your partner is sharing with you. Both should encourage the other to try new things. It is all about finding out if you are equally yoked.

Another example of a cultural difference will be the food. Food varies from country to country, and some even in the same country. Even though Italy and France are next to each other, their food is vastly different. In Italy, the food is based on the region. The northern part of Italy in the Tuscany region is very vegetable-based, while the southern heel part of the boot (Puglia region, pronounced pool-yah) is based around olives, grapes, and wheat (pasta). During your fellowship, this is a great time to explore new foods and enrich your life in another culture.

Again, if you like someone, no matter what the race or ethnic background or skin color and they like you, then give it a chance and use quality time to determine if you are equally yoked. You have to remember you are counting on God to bring you someone. Do not back away from your blessing. You cannot care more about what other people think more than what God thinks and provides. Only God knows what He has as the next step for you. God may be opening a door for you that will take you to new levels that you may not have dreamed of. He may be doing it through someone who can enrich your life and spur new ideas through this other person.

You do not want to look back and regret the relationship that you were afraid to have or the decision you waited too long to make. That good person will find someone else and you will be looking from the outside in, saying that could have been me with a good family and happy.

NOTES

DATING IN THE WORKPLACE

As Christians we should have a strong integrity and stand on our morals, values, and standards, especially when it comes to dating in the workplace. Many Christians are faced with the same situations concerning dating in the workplace as people who secularly date. You have to ask yourself: is it good to date in the workplace? As a Christian you should still take the same steps in dating in the workplace just as you would as if you were dating someone from your church. What you have to determine initially is if the other person is saved and how they view Christian dating. There are many pressures at the workplace as well as gossip. Dating where you work can be good but also difficult at the same time. I have listed some pros and cons when it comes to dating in the workplace. Dating in the workplace falls in a category of someone's opinion. Is it good or bad? Is it right or wrong?

DATING IN THE WORKPLACE

Let's start with the pros of dating someone in the workplace:

- You can see your dating partner every time you work together.
- You have time to talk to each other, which allows you to learn more about each other in a shorter time.
- You can have a conversation face-to-face rather than over the phone.
- Meeting after work can be easier because you both leave at the same time. This allows for more time in the date if you don't have to wait on the other person.
- Holiday's aren't as bad if you both have to work because you can still see each other.

Now let's look at the cons of dating someone in the workplace:

- If the other person breaks up with you, you will have to see them every time you work together.
- You may have to see them date another coworker.
- You may see the new dating partner hug, kiss, give gifts to or receive gifts from your former dating partner.
- You run the risk of the person making false claims against you if the relationship ends poorly. This could range from theft to you being physically abusive.
- The conflict doesn't have to be with a breakup either. It could be others in the workplace may

resent the fact you are dating at work, especially if you start dating a supervisor. They may feel there is favoritism with work load, scheduling, break times, etc.
- Other employees may feel you would be a supervisor's informant if you were dating a supervisor. This only brings negative attitudes to the relationship because your friends will start to turn on you.
- Gossip/rumors may start as to what you are doing in your relationship and how far you have taken the physical aspect.

There are pros and cons to dating in the work place. The cons should open you to some things you may not have thought about prior to dating someone from work. This is not meant to be a deterrent from dating at work; however, it is meant to help you keep an open and objective mind for the future.

NOTES

TEENAGE DATING

The choice is up to you and your parents, but Christian teens should still know God's perspective on dating. God has more in store for you than just jumping from one relationship to another. As a teenager, there is a lot of pressure in dating, especially pressure to have sex. This is a desire by man but brought about by temptation. Too many teenagers are hurt because they think they fall in love with a man or a woman and they find out they were used, or they were not the only guy or girl. As a teenager, you should still approach dating like an adult would in this book—no contact at all until you know what this person's motivations are. If they have distorted motivations, then move on. I know it is easier said than done, but in order to protect you and your heart, it needs to be done.

> "Above all else, guard your heart, for it is the wellspring of life."
>
> Proverbs 4:23 (NIV)

TEENAGE DATING

It's important to recognize that at sixteen, you will not have a life vision so you will need to rely on qualifying the person by other criteria. You want to look at things like what is their family life like, do they have good morals and values, does the person get along with their parents, are they looking to go to college, do they have a career interest, etc., or are they just looking for the next party or the next boy or girl.

It is not to say that any teenager reading this book will never experience heartbreak—you just do not want it to become a regular occurrence or over someone that is clearly not right for you.

Many teenagers, as well as adults, should realize your heart sometimes takes control and starts to love but a little too fast. The heart starts to love even when circumstances or certain characteristics about the person say "stay away." The heart falls in love with appearance (good looks, smells good, dresses nice), flattery, charm, confidence; but your brain sees, and to some degree acknowledges, the lack of ethics, lying, lack of employment, jealous or immature behavior, unreliability, and controlling behavior but most of the time can't override the heart.

> The heart is deceitful above all things and beyond cure. Who can understand it?
>
> Jeremiah 17:9 (NIV)

You have to understand that most of the time, when we make a bad decision, it is because we make it from a heartfelt emotion and not from a logical determination. We say "I went with my heart" even when the circumstances said not to.

As a teenager, don't be in a rush to date. You have your whole life ahead of you. If you do decide to date, take it slow. Try to evaluate who you are with, and try not to let peer pressure influence you. Your peers will not have your best interest for you; however, your parents will. Listen to your parents because they have been through the dating scene when they were your age and know what you are going through.

NOTES

INTERNET DATING

The Internet is a common way now to meet people, either through social networks or through online dating sites. I will not try to steer you one way or the other on this, it is your choice. One common thing people find about the Internet is it makes the pool of people to choose from larger. If you go to a dating site, you can also narrow down the type of persons you are looking for very easily. You can meet someone on the Internet and they can be very honest and charming or they can be just the opposite and lie about everything. No matter how you meet this person on the Internet, you should take every precaution available. Do not believe the profile on the site 100 percent. Even though we are Christians, we still need to take precautions. I understand when you go to these sites that you are looking for your perfect match. You want to believe you are going to find who you are looking for and do not want to believe someone may be lying to you. While many people find success and get married off of these sites, there are even more that find the profile to be a lie or misleading. It also goes to say it is easy to get the wrong impression from someone over the Internet. When someone writes something, you may read it differently than the way the writer intended it to be read.

One thing some online dating sites are providing is an online webcam chat feature. This allows you to talk with the person and ask questions beforehand. Take the time to do this. If you are going the route of Internet dating, spend the few extra minutes via the webcam.

If you choose to go this route, then still take the precautions I have provided book under the "Dating Tips and Guidelines for Safety" section. Most importantly, do not be by yourself with the other person and do not give out your personal information until you know them well.

DON'T LEAD ANYONE ON

This should be a no brainer as a Christian but it still happens either intentionally or unintentionally. Like we discussed in "The Goal" chapter, what is our intent? That needs to be put on the table right up front. Two people can be friends and even go out and get lunch or dinner together as friends. But again that falls in the friend or companion role, not in the getting-to-know-someone-for-potential-marriage role.

One day, I asked a very attractive lady from church out to get some ice cream with me. We had been friends for some time and got along well so she said she would like that. It was after the third time we went out she caught on that I had taken a slight liking to her and she let me know up front that she did not have any interest in dating and she did not want to lead me on. She felt it would be wrong for her to keep going out with me if I have an interest toward getting to know her more and she did not have the same interest. She felt that if we kept going out I may get attached emotionally to her and that was not the direction she was looking to go in. You see, she was looking to fellowship as friends and not looking for anything more. She said something immediately when she realized we were not yoked the same way. This was a prime example of how to handle a situation correctly, respectfully, and in a Christian way.

An example of what not to do would be when two people start to fellowship and one person has an interest in getting married and having kids someday but the other person does not. Let us say the man does not want to get married and has expressed that he only wants to go out and be friends and definitely does not want kids. It is important for him to convey that to the lady because the more she fellowships with him, the more she will think he is changing his mind and coming around to the idea that marriage and kids are good. The longer the fellowship lasts, the more that idea sets in. She will start making plans in her head of what the family life will be like. The longer this goes on, the more emotionally attached she will get and when the subject comes up again, she will be devastated that the man still does not want to get married and they have been seeing each other for a number of months.

Again, when the man decided he did not want to get married and the lady did want to get married, she was under a false impression that their relationship was going in the direction she wanted. He may not think he is leading her on. He may think he told her he wanted to be just friends but when she says she wants more and a lot more, if she wants marriage and kids then they need to understand they are unequally yoked. This type of relationship only ends badly for the person wanting to get married. This is an unintentional lead on but should have been recognized when they were not equally yoked from the beginning.

Several things play into this second example. The first is if the man has no intention of getting married, he needs to make it clear and reiterate on a regular basis that he does not want to get married or have kids. This should be reciprocated by the female if that is the intention. He needs to make it clear that they are only friends for these reasons: First, anyone who is looking to get married is always looking to further their relationship with the other person. The longer the fellowship goes on for, the more they feel the relationship is progressing. Second, when the person finds out after many months of fellowshipping that they are not any closer to getting married, they will feel they have wasted all their time when they could have been looking for or found someone else.

The person may also feel used if they have vested time, money, or both into that person's life to benefit them as a couple. If they fellowship for some time and they are spending time at each other's house, they will start to operate as a couple in the house. This does not mean sexual relations. But as time goes on, if the décor of the house changes, they will have input from the other person. In this case, the female would think even more that they are moving forward as a couple because he is asking her opinion about the décor of his house. She will feel this is a couple's decision. There may be a time when she is buying things for the house. She may feel used when the man says again that he just wants to be friends because she may be investing time and money into his house expecting it to be her house one day. Keep in mind nothing appears wrong to either of them while this is going on. They just have different ideas of what is going on in their relationship. He thinks she is just being a friend and she thinks they are moving toward marriage. They may have stated their intentions in the beginning of the fellowship, but once they moved further into the fellowship, the initial statements become faint and almost obsolete. Again, all the more reasons to stop the fellowship once you have determined you are not equally yoked. You can still be friends and, with a group, go places, but on an individual basis, it is not recommended.

Another example of what not to do would be accepting large gifts. Let us say both want to get married but the man thinks the relationship is farther along than the woman does. If he is investing his time to find her nice gifts and purchasing them for her and she receives it with open arms, this is an indication things are good in their relationship. Remember, as Christians, we have already established companionship versus marriage up front, so by this time, when the gifts start coming, the man has a vested interest in the lady. If the lady receives the gifts and keeps receiving them over time, this only tells the man she is good with their relationship. But when the day comes and he says lets step it up and get engaged and she says no or if at any point in time she decides to fellowship with another man, this will only hurt him more because he will feel mislead. Communication of where your relationship is at is very important. If the person receiving the gifts does not feel the same way about the person giving the gifts, they need to say up front they think the person is moving too fast and respectfully decline the gift.

The third type of lead on is when you fellowship with someone for the first time and everything goes great, but then they keep putting off the second fellowship. If there is a legitimate reason for you or the other person not being able to fellowship then that reason should be conveyed. If you feel the need to put the fellowship off because you are not sure if this person is the right person, then you need to fellowship that much more to determine if they are or not so you can move forward either way. If they were too strong on the first date or too much of anything then you need to convey that. It's okay to tell them you think they are a good person, but they came off to strong, overdid the jokes, or that you thought they were trying too hard to impress you. They will respect your opinion and feel more comfortable on the next fellowship. They may be a great person but nervous on the first date and just came off the wrong way. It's like judging a book by its cover. Telling someone you like them but keeping putting them off is not the right way to let someone know you do not have an interest. Communication is going to be your strongest attribute.

Another way someone may unintentionally lead someone on is by giving excuses. This is where you may not be dating or fellowshipping, but someone may ask you out for lunch or dinner and you give the excuse "I don't have time." The excuse only goes so far because if someone you really liked asked you out, you would find time to do something even for a short while. Then you have basically lied to the other person just so you didn't have to go out with them or tell them the truth. When you find that you are giving people excuses like "I don't have time," "I'm sick," "I told my parents I would visit them that day," "I can't find a babysitter," "I have no gas to drive anywhere," etc., then you are just making excuses, which should not happen. When the other person finds out you are dating someone else, it will give them a bitter feeling because you found time for the other person. Letting them know upfront that you do not want to date is okay. You can let them know that you are flattered and that they are very nice but you are not attracted to them that way. This makes for no confusion. They will not come back in a week or two and ask, "Do you have time now?" Plus, you have a clear conscience that you did the right thing. In the Bible, the scripture says if you know what is right and you do not do it then it is sin. As a Christian, you should be honest with others as well as yourself. It will also let them move on and seek the person God has intended for them. This section is not intended to say that you would be the only one making excuses, it is for you to be able to identify someone else making excuses as well.

> So any person who knows what is right to do but does not do it, to him it is sin.
>
> James 4:17 (AMP)

I also want to address the person who wanted to see more out of the relationship. When you are fellowshipping/dating someone and it does not work out, you need to turn to God even more. Not everyone will be equally yoked. Do not go through the "could've been, should've been" phase. This is where you will try to make sense out of your relationship if things happened a different way. When you start saying things like "If I would have only done that" or "If this wouldn't have happened" or "I should've said this." The fact of the matter is things did happen the way they did and you cannot change what happened. You can only move forward. How you move forward is up to you. Trying to find someone you are equally yoked with sounds like the best cure to me. Dwelling on the "could've, should've, would've" for months or years only wastes time and prevents you from finding true happiness with your real spouse. If someone has ended a relationship where they feel they are not equally yoked with you then you probably are not yoked. It is not one thing that moved you apart, it is based on several issues that should have been identified early. If it was based on one thing then you should thank God that it happened early in the relationship and not when you were a year or so into it. Any time someone says it is because of one thing, then thank God now because that person is not willing to fight for a relationship if things get tough.

Let us further this line of thought. Do not revisit the fellowship/dating if you have determined that one wants to get married and the other person does not! Even if you spend some time apart from each other and you become friends again and the hurt has dissipated, revisiting the fellowship starts those feelings again. Even if the man says he just wants to be friends right up front this time, the lady will hold on to the hope he will change his mind and will pass on every potential husband that comes by because she wants to be submissive to the man she is fellowshipping with. This is an unintentional lead on that should not happen.

I remember that one time I was trying to fellowship with a girl and she was always having trouble finding a babysitter for her kids. We went out one time and had a great time. We had a lot in common and laughed the majority of the night. When I called her for a second fellowship, she kept telling me she could not find a babysitter. One night, I called her and she said she was at the mall with her cousin. Now that immediately drew a red flag to me because she had kept saying she could not find a babysitter for us to go out. So I tried again the next week and she said she could not find a babysitter, but again when I called to talk, she said she was over her cousin's house. Then I gave it one more shot, I called her on a Sunday after church and she said she was fellowshipping with some guys from her old church. This was clearly identified as an excuse to not go out. It was an unintentional lead-on. She didn't know how to tell me that she did not have that same kind of interest in me that I had in her. When you find yourself playing around with excuses then you are lying to yourself and the other person. If you find the other person is doing that to you then you can choose to address the issue or just let it go and move on. You cannot force the person to like you. Even if they go out with you again, will they have more excuses after the second fellowship? It's not to say they will always have excuses, but it will take a longer time for you to develop trust with them.

As a Christian, you should want everyone who is looking for a husband or wife to find who they are looking for. I believe that if you have identified a person who is looking for a relationship different than what you are looking for, then you need to communicate to the other person that you are not interested in that form of relationship. If you choose to fellowship with someone and you know you are not equally yoked and they want more from the relationship, then you are doing them a disservice because they have you in their focus and will not entertain anyone else if they think they have a chance with you. If you let it go for any amount of time, you may be unintentionally leading them on. They may be okay with fellowshipping for a year or two or three, but in that time, they could have found a person that would suit them as a spouse. I have heard both men and women say that they wasted their time with someone who never had any intention of getting married. Some have gone on to say the other person stole their youthful years. As a Christian, if you know what type of relationship someone is looking for and you know you are not the person to fulfill that role, then it is up to you to not lead them on and let them find the person God has for them.

NOTES

DATING AFTER A BAD RELATIONSHIP

This section is here for those who have had bad relationships and are trying to get back into a good relationship. Let us start by giving a short analysis of what not to do.

First, do not compare a new dating partner with the ex-partner. The new person has not done anything to you and you should not microanalyze this new relationship. When you start to microanalyze the relationship, you show your distrust and that is not a good foundation to build on. You will start to read into something that is not there and make bad decisions based on distrust from your past relationship.

Second, it is important that those feelings are expressed and that they are expressed clearly. Trust takes time to develop, especially after a bad relationship. See "Developing Trust" section

Third, take the new relationship slow. You have to be comfortable with yourself and be happy with yourself before you can see the goodness that can come from another person. If you are not comfortable with yourself, then you will always question why they are doing what they are doing, and then saying they must be trying something that your ex did too. Take it slow and talk with the person. Let them know your feelings. If you do not communicate, then they will not know what is bothering you. It will also make it hard for them to support you or help you when you are having trouble.

DOES AGE MATTER?

Does age matter when it comes to dating? Again, this is an individual preference, but let me try to open up your mind on this subject. If you are leaning on God to provide you with a good Christian person and God provides someone for you, why does age matter? If you say I will not date anyone outside five years of my age and God provides someone that is seven years younger or older, why does it matter? If you are equally yoked with someone and both of you are being true to yourself and the other person, then why does age matter? This is a topic that only you can make that decision of what you want to do. I believe when you put too many limits on what you want then you become close minded and will not see the glory of what God has for you. Again, let us take age for example. God provides you with a person that is a year or two younger than what your tolerance is but their vision is right in line with yours, they want to move the kingdom forward like you do, they are attractive to you and may even be in the "hot" category, they are fun to be around, they know their

Bible, they are good with prayer, but you say they do not fall into your age acceptance. Would someone really pass up a lifetime of happiness and blessings because the other person was just outside their age range? What about ten years' or more difference? If you are yoked with someone, what does age matter? My point behind this is not to say you should be looking for someone fifteen years younger than you, it is to say keep an open mind when God puts someone in front of you.

In some of the discussions that I have had with people, they say they do not want to date anyone too young because they are ready to settle down and a younger person is still too wild, they are afraid the younger person will find someone their own age later on, they do not want to feel like they are dating someone who could be their kid, and the list goes on. Those are all great discussion point when you are in the flesh. Those are also all points that show you are not equally yoked too. Remember, we are trying to find God's best for us so we can be married for a lifetime. Finding someone you are equally yoked with should take precedent over age. The call is yours and only yours. I hope this section helped with any questions you may have had on age difference.

ENDING A RELATIONSHIP

Fellowshipping and dating can be a joyful experience, but it can also be a challenging experience. You try to do everything you can during the relationship to make things work so if there is ever a time you determine you are not equally yoked with the other person, there is not a doubt in your mind that you made the right decision to end the relationship.

How do you know if you are not equally yoked with the other person? There are a great number of reasons why you may not be equally yoked, but to list each one would be an entire set of books. What you need to do is ask yourself several questions, such as:

- Does this person bless me? (Spiritually, financially, intellectually, emotionally, etc.)
- Do I find myself arguing with this person more than I find joy with them?

ENDING A RELATIONSHIP

- Is there constant stress surrounding my relationship?
- Has our interests changed?
- Was I under the wrong impression of the person I was fellowshipping with?
- Am I attracted to this person physically or spiritually anymore?
- Do I feel like I am being dragged down or fatigued because of the relationship?
- Do I feel used? (Money, transportation, food, expenses, etc.)
- Do I feel mistreated?
- Do I feel the other person is untrustworthy?
- Is the other person inconsiderate toward my feelings?

These are questions you will need to answer honestly to determine if you are not equally yoked with the other person. There is nothing wrong with ending a fellowship if you feel you are not equally yoked. You should do it in a respectful manner and caring way. Remember that communication is a strong point in the relationship. Being able to sit down with someone and tell them the relationship is over is the right thing to do. As a Christian, you should not break up with someone via text message, voicemail, note, mutual friend, or by avoidance. Give the person some respect and articulate why you are not equally yoked. Being open to them will allow them to understand and have closure to the relationship. They may not like it and they may be upset, but it is the best way to do so. It also leaves you with a clear conscience knowing that you did everything to determine if you were equally yoked or not and you also ended it in a dignified Christian way. Anything less will torment the person as to why the relationship ended. Sometimes when you end a relationship it can be a painful period, feelings of empathy mixed with remorse and guilt for both you and this other person. This is why you need to be 100 percent sure you are breaking up with this person for the right reasons.

Just be careful that you are not jumping ship too fast. Sometimes, another person comes into your sight and you feel they are a better match. If you decide to end the relationship, then make sure the relationship is done first and not because someone else came along. Too many times a person leaves a good relationship for the next best person and they realize after a short period of time that it was the wrong thing to do. Sometimes, a person will take you back and sometimes they won't. Sometimes, ending a relationship is clear-cut and sometimes you may struggle with it. If you are planning on ending a relationship, seek God first.

Another thing you do not want to do when you are ending a relationship is minimize your relationship with the other person. Some people will try to minimize their relationship especially if there is another person waiting in the short distance. The thinking is that it is easier to tell the new perspective partner you were only friends with your former dating partner than to say you were in a six month relationship that ended because you argued too much. If you progressed from fellowshipping to dating and at some point determined that it was not going to work out, do not use an excuse of "Well, we are only friends" or something to that effect to end the relationship. This makes the break-up more difficult for the other person because they know the truth and know both of you had vested time together. Once you established you were equally yoked enough to start dating, then end the relationship in a respectful manner as indicated above. Articulate why you are ending the relationship. Don't give an excuse that tries to minimize what your relationship was. It's about being honest with yourself and with the other person. Certainly no one wants to be hurt in a relationship, and giving the other person respect with your honesty will go much further. Wouldn't you want the other person to show you that same respect?

RECOVERING FROM A BREAKUP

When a breakup occurs, there are several different places you could be in. To break this down, are you the person who is doing the breaking up, or are you the person who is being broken up with?

If you are the person doing the breaking up, then you will have your own reasons for doing so. It doesn't mean that it will be easy. Sometimes it is painful because you see not only the parts of your relationship that were bad come to an end, but you also see parts that were good come to an end, as well. It is not easy breaking up with someone if you determine you are not yoked for marriage because you may still find them to be a good person. Most people don't like seeing a dating partner upset. They don't like seeing the person cry or in some cases get angry. Breaking up with someone is difficult on just about any level if you have had some good times together.

Sometimes there may have been very little good so the decision is easy. The big question is why didn't the relationship work out, and why can't they see things your way? Everyone likes to think they have the best way. Sometimes a person looks at another person they have an interest in and visualize what a great relationship they will have and they plan the relationship out in there head. They take it so far in their head that when reality hits, they feel like the other person is not falling in line with their plan and become angry that the person has a different view of a relationship. If you get into this phase, then it is time to talk with someone on a serious level. This is tough to get through because you have planned your future out and now have to come to the startling reality that the future may not be with this other person. This may be time to talk with close friends as well as your pastor.

You have to remember God does things for us not to us. If you go through a relationship and you determine that it needs to come to an end, you should have some learning experiences from that relationship. You should have a better understanding of what you like in a relationship and what you do not like in a relationship. You should also be able to mature in yourself and know a little more about what you should or shouldn't do in a relationship. You have to remember that God is in control. He will either allow something to happen, or He will command it to happen.

Whether you are having to end a relationship or on the other side where someone has ended the relationship with you, getting over a relationship for some people is very difficult. I want to identify different ideas that may help you get through this tough time.

One thing you should consider after a bad relationship or a painful breakup is to separate completely from each other right after the relationship has ended. This means not seeing each other, no phone calls, no e-mails, no text messages, no social media, no instant messaging, etc. In some cases even delete the phone number. This does not mean permanently, but until you feel that you can converse with him/her on a purely platonic level, without an ulterior motive.

Another idea is to put away or get rid of all the things that trigger your memory of the other person. This could be photos, personal items, CDs, a mug, a book, candles or scents that remind you of them, videos of places you went, etc. The list can go on and on. You will know these items because when you walk into a room that will hit you and you will feel that little heartache. Some things may be a little less apparent but still remove them from your sight. I say all this because the more you see these items the more you will reopen the hurt each time you walk by.

Everyone is different when it comes to how they handle the aftermath of a breakup or bad relationship. Some people want to be by themselves, some turn to food for comfort; some choose not to eat etc. It is difficult to get past on your own because the hurt becomes the focal point and not the healing. You need to be able to recognize and identify that there are two kinds of hurt. The first is the kind that will hold you down, and the second is the kind that you learn from and develop from. The first kind is where the devil wants us. The devil wants us hurt and torn down because when you are over the situation, you will want to find someone again and the devil knows the strength of a husband and wife together is stronger than just one alone. We develop from the second kind of hurt because we know God is in control and that He knows what is best for us. Sometimes, it is not revealed right away but it will be in the future. Understand that there is no benefit in holding on to heartache, regret, and hatred toward the other person. This only holds you back.

You should want good people around you who love you and who will help you feel good about yourself. Surrounding yourself with compassionate, supportive Christian friends and family will help you through the initial hurt phase of the breakup. This makes the time for recovery shorter and easier because when you feel alone, the recovery process takes longer. One thing you want to try to prevent is hanging around people who keep refueling the fire (the hurt). When you are trying to recover from a breakup or bad relationship, you need to be around people who are lifting you up, not just people who want to consistently talk about the breakup and the circumstances around it. You want to watch who you are letting speak into your life. Even though you may have mutual friends, you will want to be careful and identify what they are saying to you. If they keep talking about the other person and not knowing why they broke up with you or if they are giving you updates about the other person, those things just reopen the hurt inside. It may be wise to stay clear of some people until you feel better if they keep talking about something that opens your emotions and sets you back.

I think one of the simplest definition of a Christian friend is a friend that encourages you to do better when you are up and things are going good, and they are also the same friends that help you back up if you are down without faulting you or trying to give you unrealistic reasoning's to make you feel better when it only makes the situation hurt more.

You have to remember that God is in control. God loves you and He wants you to be happy. God wants you to seek Him first and let Him guide you. You need to be able to receive what He says. When God has your ear, He will talk to you; when He has your heart, He will minister to you. God loves you! He knows you're hurt and wants you to come to Him. You will feel so much better once your mind and heart is on God and His word.

NOTES

WHY DO YOU STAY?

One thing a person needs to look at is themselves and ask themselves what was it that made them put up with the bad relationship for so long? If you are only dating someone there is nothing tying you to them, so why stay? That question can become more complicated if you are married because God does not like divorce. It is also complicated if you are dating and have kids because not only is the relationship affecting you but it affects the kids too.

So I ask the question why stay? You should ask yourself some questions about this:

1. Do I have low self-esteem?
2. Am I scared to be by myself?
3. Will it be too tough to find someone else?
4. Will I be able to financially afford being by myself?
5. Am I afraid the other person will physically hurt me?
6. Maybe I deserve this type of relationship?

WHY DO YOU STAY?

There is no reason to stay in a bad relationship, especially if it is abusive. If you are in a relationship and need a way out, talk to your pastor. They should be able to give you advice on appropriate steps to take for your situation.

This is also a time to learn from this type of relationship. How it started, how it progressed, what to look for in the next relationship, etc. You can be certain God does not want you in a bad or abusive relationship. God loves you and wants to bless you with a beautiful relationship.

Sometimes, you have to realize that in your outer self (your flesh), you carry yourself a certain way that may attract the wrong person. But let us take this to a spiritual level. You may still have old spirits in you that are attracting a similar spirit. For example, if you were engaging in premarital sex and you have not been delivered from that spirit of temptation of the flesh, then that will be the type of spirit that you will be attracted to and ones that you will attract. Since you have not been delivered from that and you attract that type of spirit, you will find that you have the same type of relationships, just with a different person.

DON'T GO BACK

Many times after being separated from your partner, it seems almost right to go back and rekindle the relationship. When you spend some time apart from each other, the hurt has dissipated, and the bad memories become forgotten or you are willing to overlook the bad memories. My best advice is don't go back to the ex-boyfriend or ex-girlfriend once you are broken up. A large percent of the time, this is a trick by the devil to get you back together. Once you are apart from the other person, you are separated from any drama. The devil plays on that. The devil will play back only the good times in your relationship. He will play back all the fun places you went to, all the fun things you did, all the good restaurants you have eaten at, but the trouble is he only plays back the good, clearly and vividly. The bad experiences seem to get overshadowed and never really played back until you are back in the relationship wasting your time again. Then you say, "Oh, yeah, that's why we broke up." Now, I know there are people who have gone back and made a relationship work after they have broken up. Praise God and I love that they found their rib and body. However, those are few and far between. Let the ex be an ex, unless you feel God is making it happen. Just do not get that confused with your own emotion. Whatever it was that drove you apart in the past has to be clearly resolved before you decide to go back.

If you should feel that God is working in your life and you are try to rekindle the relationship, it is my recommendation that the relationship start fresh and not pick up from where you left off. Starting fresh allows you to work out those differences in the beginning without automatically putting yourself back in habits or routines you had with the person.

EVALUATING YOURSELF

Evaluate your own self-esteem. If you have a low self-esteem, you might be attracting the wrong kinds of people. Low self-esteem leads many people to accept unacceptable behavior from a prospective spouse. Some of the warning signs, which should not be ignored, include mood swings, fits of anger, inability to handle frustration, sexist jokes and behavior, overly controlling behavior, and lack of consideration for the feelings of you or others.

Does your date insult you or demean you in front of friends? Do they pressure you for sex or ask to take nude or sexual photos? Abuse alcohol or drugs? If you are attracting or tolerating these kinds of people, this is a good time to seek counseling from your pastor.

This is why in Proverbs 4:14-15 (NIV) the scripture says: "Do not set foot on the path of the wicked or walk in the way of evildoers. Avoid it, do not travel on it; turn from it and go on your way." You don't want to let anyone talk you into doing something that is immoral and of a sinful nature. They will be the ones who will keep you depressed, with low self-esteem, or searching for the only thing God can give you.

You will also want to be open to what the pastor or counselor has to say constructively. If you are tolerating things in a relationship that should not be tolerated, then you will want to have an open mind, listen, and apply what your pastor or counselor is telling you. They want to see you with the true blessing God has for you. If you are tolerating certain acts by other people then you need to listen to someone who will give you good advice, pray with you, and provide a way to see you through this difficult time.

GETTING YOURSELF TOGETHER

We rely on God all the time, but sometimes we block out what God is telling us to do for ourselves. God may be telling you that you need to work on yourself first before he blesses you with a new partner. This could range anywhere from developing your knowledge of the Bible to developing a better prayer life. He may also be saying take better care of yourself, get in better shape, eat better, take vitamins; all in all, become healthier. Our bodies are God's temple, after all.

> Don't you know that you yourselves are God's temple and that God's Spirit dwells in your midst?
>
> If anyone destroys God's temple, God will destroy that person; for God's temple is sacred, and you together are that temple.
>
> 1 Corinthians 3:16–17 (NIV)

He may be saying you need to dress better, develop better hygiene habits, and smell better. After all, who wants to sit next to a bad smelling person if you can smell them from two rows away, let alone have a relationship with them? You may be blocking your own blessing! I say this because God may be telling you that you need to develop a little more and not the person He is going to pair you with.

Let me give you an example. If I have faith in God to bring me a beautiful wife but I sit at home and never leave, I may be blocking my blessing because I will never interact with anyone except at my door. God will say I need to do more than just wait! I have to take some initiative in this too.

Nobody wants to sit next to anyone who does not look nice, smell nice, or take care of themselves. If your hygiene says stay away, then guess what, people will stay away! If your appearance is inviting then you are more approachable. Now, do not blow this out of proportion. When I say look better, smell better, dress better, etc., that does not mean get into the flesh and spend all your money on $5000 suits or skimpy clothes. It means just look nice and smell nice. Do not put all your money into appearance or go overboard. We do not want to put anything in front of God. I think it is important to remember that while we are looking for God's best, so is the person God is trying to pair us up with. If you do not take care of yourself, then how high are you setting that standard for the person trying to find you? Remember, everyone is searching for God's best, not who can spend the most money.

Another part that God may be telling you to get yourself together is taking the negative feelings and thoughts out of your life. He may be saying get yourself together mentally. Too many people walk around with a negative spirit to them that can be caused by anything—work, prior relationship, family, money, etc. These things need to be recognized and turned over to God. If you are expecting God's best but you are not going to give your best because you are being held back due to outside circumstances, then it is time to deal with those negative circumstances and influences. Once you take care of the negative things in your life, it leaves a whole lot more room for you to be more positive. Dealing with the negative aspects of your life is even more important as a Christian because you are connected with the Holy Spirit. How do you think or expect the Holy Spirit to flow though you if you have all that negative energy bottled up inside.

This is also a time to try to work on any negative feelings if you are a person who waits for the other shoe to drop. We call this "breaking familiar spirits" for those who have the same reoccurring situation with the same results. Many times if a person is broken up with over and over instead of doing the breaking up, they become conditioned that when they do start seeing someone new, they expect the other shoe to drop or in other terms wait for the person to break up with them. That is not the way to start a relationship. When you wait for the other shoe to drop, it shows in your confidence or lack thereof. You may not see it yourself but the other person can see it. It is not something that someone normally points out to another person; they just see it as a lack of confidence or a behavior that they are not attracted to. My best advice is if you are seeking God first and God put a person in front of you, use this book and the teachings in it to help you qualify the person. You will be able to see your self-esteem develop and be able to continue your relationships more confidently. This comes from renewing your mind on a daily basis. You can find this in Romans 12:2.

As a man, God is expecting you to get a job if possible before He blesses you with a great wife. After all, he did the same with Adam. God had Adam tending to the Garden of Eden and he had to name all of the living creatures on earth before God created Eve.

> And the Lord God took the man, and put him into the garden of Eden to dress it and to keep it.
>
> And the Lord God said, It is not good that the man should be alone; I will make him an help meet for him.
>
> And out of the ground the Lord God formed every beast of the field, and every fowl of the air; and brought them unto Adam to see what he would call them: and whatsoever Adam called every living creature, that was the name thereof.
>
> And Adam gave names to all cattle, and to the fowl of the air, and to every beast of the field; but for Adam there was not found an help meet for him.
>
> And the Lord God caused a deep sleep to fall upon Adam, and he slept: and he took

> one of his ribs, and closed up the flesh instead thereof;
> And the rib, which the Lord God had taken from man, made he a woman, and brought her unto the man.
>
> Genesis 2:15, 18–22

Side note: If you have been relying on God for some time to bring you your perfect person, you may and probably will encounter various people that will try to give you helpful tips on what you are doing wrong and try to justify why you have not found anyone yet. They will tell you that you are too picky, your standards are too high, you need to broaden the range of people you are attracted to, etc. While in some cases they may be right, only you can hear from God and what He is telling you. The teachings I received were to listen to God and know God will bring someone to me.

One day, an Elder was telling me that I set my standards too high and that I am too picky. I said, "How's that?" I am looking for a woman who believes and loves God. I said I do not limit my choices to one particular race. I have a broad range of what I find attractive in a woman. I said I do not put a standard on their knowledge of the Bible just that they like to learn more which I did not think was unreasonable. He said "there must be something else wrong." He said I should try looking outside the church. I told him all avenues are open and that God told me to be patient. I realized because I was not dating someone serious in his timeframe he thought something was wrong. I told this testimony to say this: When God tells you to be patient, then just be patient! Do not live by someone else's timetable. I was not dating someone for a long time because when I identified that I was not equally yoked with someone, I stopped the fellowship. I realized that some people would keep dating just to have someone around until the next best thing came. I do not do that. I also did not want to delay the woman God had for me based on my selfish actions of just wanting to have someone around. I practice what I have preached in this book. If you have been waiting a while for someone then you need to put God in your heart and listen to Him. You just have to be patient. The longer you wait, the better the person God has for you. I also believe that God will be doing something way bigger for you than what you realize and he wants you to be ready for the person he brings to you because you will have a bigger purpose than what you think in the kingdom.

> Wait for the LORD;
> be strong and take heart
> and wait for the LORD.
>
> Psalm 27:14 (NIV)

WHAT IS LOVE?

So the question is "What is Love?" Well, we can find a definition of love in the Bible from 1 Corinthians 13. It tells us how, without love, there is nothing.

> If I could speak all the languages of earth and of angels, but didn't love others, I would only be a noisy gong or a clanging cymbal.
>
> If I had the gift of prophecy, and if I understood all of God's secret plans and possessed all knowledge, and if I had such faith that I could move mountains, but didn't love others, I would be nothing.
>
> If I gave everything I have to the poor and even sacrificed my body, I could boast about it; but if I didn't love others, I would have gained nothing.
>
> Love is patient and kind. Love is not jealous or boastful or proud or rude. It does not demand its own way. It is not irritable, and it keeps no record of being wronged.

WHAT IS LOVE?

> It does not rejoice about injustice but rejoices whenever the truth wins out. [7] Love never gives up, never loses faith, is always hopeful, and endures through every circumstance.
>
> Love never gives up, never loses faith, is always hopeful, and endures through every circumstance.
>
> 1 Corinthians 13:1–7

A very good book that talks about loving yourself and loving God and gives a complete breakdown of 1 Corinthians 13:1-7 is a book called *Love Perfect* by L.G. Gurley.

We can also find an example of true love, unconditional love, in John 3:16 and John 4:10–11.

> "For God loved the world so much that he gave his one and only Son, so that everyone who believes in him will not perish but have eternal life.
>
> John 3:16

> This is real love—not that we loved God, but that he loved us and sent his Son as a sacrifice to take away our sins.
>
> Dear friends, since God loved us that much, we surely ought to love each other.
>
> 1 John 4:10–11

You can see from these scriptures that God loves us unconditionally. God saw that not only do we as humans sin but we were born into sin so "He sent His one and only Son, so that everyone who believes in

Him will not perish but have eternal life." Jesus came to die for our sins. Keep in mind His death was not a death where he laid down and fell asleep, never to wake up, but it was a brutal death. The beatings and punishment Jesus took for us was like no other. Only Jesus could take that kind of punishment for the world. Plain and simple, that is love!

> "You have heard the law that says, 'Love your neighbor' and hate your enemy.
> But I say, love your enemies! Pray for those who persecute you!
> In that way, you will be acting as true children of your Father in heaven. For he gives his sunlight to both the evil and the good, and he sends rain on the just and the unjust alike.
> If you love only those who love you, what reward is there for that? Even corrupt tax collectors do that much.
> If you are kind only to your friends, how are you different from anyone else? Even pagans do that.
>
> Matthew 5:43–47 (NLT)

> Be completely humble and gentle; be patient, bearing with one another in love.
>
> Ephesians 4:2 (NIV)

Since we are created in the image of God and God loves us unconditionally, then we should love people too. This means helping others in need, not doing so out of obedience but out of the joy of helping. We have all been put in a position at one time or another where we said "If I could just get a break!" You are doing something good out of the fruit of the spirit, not out of seeking something in return.

> Do nothing out of selfish ambition or vain conceit. Rather, in humility value others above yourselves,
>
> Philippians 2:3 (NIV)

God shows us in John 4:18 that love is important because it expels out fear.

> "Such love has no fear, because perfect love expels all fear."
>
> 1John 4:18

Last and foremost, 1 Corinthians 13:13 spells it out for us where love ranks.

> And now these three remain: faith, hope and love. But the greatest of these is love.
>
> 1 Corinthians 13:13 (NIV)

We express love in many ways, both verbally and physically, but you need to understand the tongue has no bones but it is one of the strongest parts of your body. Be careful of your words and how you use them. You want to be encouraging and plant good seed. You do not know what someone will hold on to for the rest of their life. Speak out of love. Anything else is not of God and can have a negative impact in someone's life.

> Death and life are in the power of the tongue:
> and they that love it shall eat the fruit thereof."
>
> Proverbs 18:21 (KJV)

You can say the words I love you or you can say you are sorry. You can say whatever you want whenever you want, but if your actions are not meeting your words, then your words are meaningless.

Since this book is on dating, you should be looking at how to show love toward your partner. As you learn about your partner, you will see the things they desire, whether tangible things or things you do for them. It is very important to keep those things in mind and act on them throughout your relationship and marriage.

The one thing you cannot do is put your own personal agenda above your relationship. Any time you put the love of hobbies or your desire for tangible things over your relationship, then you are becoming in the flesh and you are moving away from loving your partner. This is especially important in marriage because then you start to look at your spouse only in a romantic way, which if the romance stops, then you feel you are not compatible anymore. You need to make your spouse the "subject of your love," not the "object of your lust." That is a powerful statement! Everything you do should be out of love for the other person. You work out of love to provide for the household, you do things around the house out of love to make the house comfortable for each other, you do things outside and go places out of love for life enrichment. You do these things out of love just like you do your best out of love to please

WHAT IS LOVE?

God. Anytime you fall away from love and your spouse becomes the focal point only when a romantic desire hits, then you need to reevaluate your selfish desires and focus on your family values.

> Dear children, let's not merely say that we love each other; let us show the truth by our actions.
>
> 1 John 3:18 (NLT)

When you say the words "I love you," they should mean just that. The term "I love you" should not be used as a general reply if someone has said it to you first. It should not be used to try and further a relationship if it is not meant or to appease the other person. When you say "I love you," it means "I love you," and that means you are committed and can see your future with this person.

WHAT THE BIBLE SAYS ABOUT SEX

So we have talked a lot about how to get to know someone in order to see if they match up with you on every level. You know you should be able to communicate well with each other, your visions line up, your love for God is the same, and you have determined that this is a person that you are willing to spend the rest of your life with, both physically and spiritually. Throughout the fellowship, dating, and engagement portions of your relationship, you will be faced with the temptation of sex. This section will open up the scriptures that talk about sex and I will expand on it as well.

Is it okay to have sex before marriage? The answer is no! Having premarital sex is not in the will of God as we can see here in 1 Corinthians 7:2.

> But because of the temptation to sexual immorality, each man should have his own wife and each woman her own husband."
>
> 1 Corinthians 7:2

This clearly shows God intends for us to be married prior to having sex.

As we can see here in 1 Corinthians 6:18, having sex before marriage is a sin against your own body. This is important because when you have sex, you become spiritually connected with that person.

> Flee from sexual immorality. Every other sin a person commits is outside the body, but the sexually immoral person sins against his own body."
>
> 1 Corinthians 6:18

> Marriage should be honored by all, and the marriage bed kept pure, for God will judge the adulterer and all the sexually immoral."
>
> Hebrews 13:4

Abstaining from sex is a difficult thing, both for man and woman. It is an act that is very pleasurable that everyone wants to experience. It is also an act that God has intended for married people. Everyone needs to understand that you become married in the spirit when you have sex. Sometimes, people forget about spiritual bond that comes with sex. It becomes difficult to abstain when there is no one physically watching your every move. But what people sometimes forget is that God is always watching.

Let's talk about what happens in the flesh. There are too many negatives that come out of having sex that do not get talked about or are tolerated. Sex outside of marriage leads to pregnancy and life changes. We all know that sex can lead to pregnancy. Often, it leads to unwanted pregnancy. If you are one of the lucky women who finds a man that will marry you or wants to help you support the baby, consider yourself lucky because it does not happen too often. I will detail some of those changes below:

LIFESTYLE CHANGES

Life style change #1: Priority rearrangement: Babies are twenty-four-hour responsibilities. No more just getting up and hanging out at the friend's house, being out late, sleeping in or sleeping through the night etc. If you choose to go out, you need a babysitter, which costs money.

Life style change #2: Money: Kids are not free. They take lots of money to raise, starting with all the supplies you will need to buy such as car seat, crib (pad, linens, etc.), diapers and diaper supplies (diaper rash cream, lotion, oil, baby powder, etc.), baby wipes, changing pad, diaper bag, clothing (including winter wear if applicable), special laundry detergent, breastfeeding equipment, bottle feeding items, medicines plus bouncers or swings, just to name a few things but the list goes on.

Life style change #3: Money part 2: Daycare and a babysitting. Depending on the parts that you live in, daycare can be $800 or more per month per child. Not only do you have the extra financial responsibilities, but now you have to incorporate time to go and pick them up and drop them off.

This is tough if you are married, but when you are single it is very tough. There is no more going home right after work and taking a nap or stopping by the friends for a couple hours, etc. You also have the responsibility to find a responsible sitter who will take care of your child, who will keep them safe and feed them as they require. You would not turn your kid over to someone who would harm them, right?

Life style change #4: Food and dietary restrictions: Once you have a child and decide to breastfeed, you will need to watch your food intake. You cannot eat spicy foods, drink any alcohol (if they are used to doing so), and basically anything that can be passed onto the baby through breastfeeding.

Life style change #5: Health: As a parent, you do not become immune to colds, flu, or any other illness that comes around. Now, you are taking care of your child and yourself. This means that you may have to take time off work, which means you do not get paid; again, going back to point number two—kids are not free.

Life style change #6: Child Support: Child support, while designed to help the parent with custody of their child, does not always work smoothly or fairly to some. Checks can be late or, God forbid, you are the mother of child number four or five by this man. Primary child support goes to the first child. You may be lucky to receive anything if you are that far down the list of mothers with kids by this man. You become more of a statistic and that does not pay the bills.

Life style change #7: Emotional Standpoint: There are many women that get emotionally scarred because they loved a man, got pregnant, and then he leaves. A lot of women get over that particular scar and move on to another man. When the cycle hits three and four kids, the woman becomes bitter to all men, saying there are no good men out there or they feel the system owes them or someone owes them. The common denominator in this is premarital sex.

This topic can be a whole book in itself. I ask women to evaluate the man they are with. You have a lifetime with this man if he is meant for you. While children are a blessing, they are not easy to raise. You never want to abort a baby so this is why it is easier to be proactive to resisting sex rather than reactive and having to raising a child.

Guys, I am not leaving you out either. Stop trying to talk women into sex. Find yourself a good woman that you can have a future with. The drawbacks for a guy are bad as well. Some women will make allegations of rape once they find out you don't want to support the child or that you want to leave. God forbid that any of this happens in a Christian relationship. As the father of a baby you will also owe child support. This means you will be paying money for the next 18 years. When you do meet a lady that you want to be your wife, you are already starting your relationship off in hardship. Your extra money will be allocated elsewhere. If you plan on skipping child support and you miss a couple of payments, a delinquency notice will be sent out to you. This only becomes more of a headache because you are on the courts radar now. If you do not respond and the account continues to accumulate, then a warrant for arrest can be issued. Just what you need is jail time, right? Kids grow up way too often without a father in their household. Being a Christian man, you need to take care of your responsibilities.

Often, in the beginning of a relationship, you wish you knew everything about the person. What both men and women also need to understand about a sexual relationship is when sex drives the relationship and one person determines they do not want to see the other person, it can lead to the burden of them calling all the time. They may not leave you alone, or they may even try to break up your new relationship. Some people even go as far as stalking the other person. Sex is a powerful spirit and can do more harm than good if you are not married. Once someone has experienced the good feeling with you, then they do not want to give it up. Not only do they not want to give it up, they definitely do not want anyone else to experience that same feeling with you that they did. It can drive some people to do some crazy, irrational things, even becoming violent. It goes with the old saying "Be careful of what you wish for!" You just might get your wish and find out everything about them, including how bad their temperament is and if they can become violent.

Another thing that you have to think about now in today's age is who wants to have sex with you? You have to consider how many other people they are sleeping with as well. If they have three partners and each partner has three other partners, the probability of contracting a disease is very good. Now, I understand that we are Christians and by God's word we are not to have sex and I am not trying to imply anyone specific is, but that temptation of sex even happens to Christians. Not just the newly saved but any Christians. It is a matter of how you handle it.

Let us take the teaching into a different direction. I heard this joke one time that goes like this:

> Question: What kind of food stops a person's sex drive?
>
> Answer: Wedding Cake

Everybody has heard that when you get married, the sex drive stops, or is substantially reduced. The devil wants you to have sex all the time before you get married, "all the time!" The idea of the devil is for you to have sex as much as you can before you get married, then, as a result, he puts a bind on you and your spouse so the sex drive will stop when you are married. Only when you are married is when it is in God's will for you to have sex. Do not let the devil into your life like that and do not let the devil bind your marriage.

I say all this because you really need to follow the Bible and what it says. Abstain from sex and get married first before you have your family. I understand people do not like to hear that, but it is the best biblically and is the best form of birth control. It is best for your future marriage and for your future family.

NOTES

FILTERING OUT TEMPTATIONS

Getting rid of the temptations that we can control plays a big part every time we are with the other person. Now, I say the temptations we can control. There are temptations of the eye that you cannot control like sporadic things on the TV. We understand that those things we just turn away from when it happens, but the things we can control are our focus. First, you need to get rid of the magazines that take your mind into desire. Now, I am not talking about pornographic material specifically but magazines that are still somewhat revealing that stimulate your mind in that direction. This also goes for viewing videos and the Internet, any videos that have explicit material—again, it does not have to be pornographic but something that stimulates your mind. If you are on the Internet and you are viewing photos of people you do not know wearing next to nothing then you are taking your mind into what is considered pleasurable or lust. These things stimulate your mind and make you weaker when you are confronted for real in the flesh because you have been activating that desire mentally. Even if you are not dating someone, it still holds the same weight because it is a lustful act. Are there exceptions? Sure, say if someone you know has been battling a weight loss problem and they post a picture of their results, complimenting them is not inappropriate. It is being supportive of their accomplishment. Getting rid of the outside temptations first keeps your mind where it needs to be—on God and not in lust. If you are a person that says it does not stimulate you, then why do you look at it? To put it in the big picture, is what you are doing honoring or glorifying God in any way?

You have to remember the devil is slick. The devil does not come in the form of a devil with horns and a red pitchfork. He comes as something inviting and talks to you, trying to get you to think everything is okay. The devil says, "What's the harm in looking at some photos or videos?" The devil will tempt you, and there comes that good feeling, you see the hot body and say, "Mmm…they look good." The devil tempts you just as he did when he tempted Eve with the fruit from the Tree of Knowledge. In Genesis 3:6, the scripture says she was convinced it was okay to eat! You see the devil did his job. The devil made Eve doubt God's word. Then you see in Genesis 3:13, Eve realizes and says, "The serpent deceived me…," but by this point it was already too late.

Anytime you get into lustful acts, it creates a thought process that when confronted for real in the flesh it makes it harder to turn away from. You have to recognize the devil's tactics when they come. Photos and videos are the fastest way to get your mind into that lustful mode because you can do that in private where you say nobody will know. Then, when you are confronted with the hot body in front of you, it is much harder to turn away from sex because your mind has been stimulated from all the other photos, videos, multimedia, etc. My best advice is to get rid of the temptations that you can control.

This is why in the New Testament, in 1 Peter 4, lust is associated with what pagans do. Do you really want to be associated with what pagans do? Do not let the devil twist your thoughts. Once you recognize it, turn away from it.

> "Therefore, since Christ suffered in his body, arm yourselves also with the same attitude, because whoever suffers in the body is done with sis a result, they do not live the rest of their earthly lives for evil human desires, but rather for the will of God. For you have spent enough time in the past doing what pagans choose to do—living in debauchery, *lust*, drunkenness, orgies, carousing and detestable idolatry."
>
> 1 Peter 4:1–3 (NIV)
> [emphasis mine]

Temptations also happen in other areas too. They happen in gambling, drinking, drugs, etc. The closer you get to temptation, the closer you get to committing the act. Gambling, drinking, and drugs are not a direct form of dating but can put a strain on your relationship.

SIMPLE PRAYER

Lord, I come to you in the name of Jesus. I loose myself of all relationships that are of the flesh and not the spirit. Lord, help me resist all sexual impurities, lust, pornography, sexual desires, and any negative impurity that encompasses sexual immorality. I pray that I am cleansed from my past and my past now stays in the past. That nothing will hinder my present and future. I pray for strength to keep my mind pure, and by body whole. I pray that any and all negative emotions and thoughts from past relationship dissipate so I can be healed. In Jesus's name. Amen.

FAITH: MINI SERMON

Every Christian needs to develop a strong foundation of faith. This is imperative for your relationships and development as a Christian. There are many scriptures on faith and why it is important to have. In this section, I have highlighted a few faith scriptures and expanded on why faith is important and gave biblical examples of people with unconditional faith in the Bible.

WHERE DOES FAITH COME FROM?

> "So then faith cometh by hearing, and hearing by the word of God."

Here we see the scripture saying "hearing by the word of God." This brings me back to when my pastor would tell me to read my Bible. If you do not read the word, you will have no faith; read the word a little and have little faith; get the word in abundance and have lots of faith. This does not mean to only read your Bible either; it means going to church and hear the word being spoken.

Christians live by faith and not by fear. Notice I did not say they "should" live by faith and without fear. We live by faith and not by fear. If God stands before us than who can stand against us? The Devil's number one goal is for us to doubt God's word. He wants us to live in fear. The more you live in fear, the farther you get away from the kingdom, the harder it is to advance the kingdom forward and brings you closer to the world.

> Now faith is the assurance (the confirmation, the title deed) of the things [we] hope for, being the proof of things [we] do not see and the conviction of their reality [faith perceiving as real fact what is not revealed to the senses].
>
> Hebrews 11:1 (AMP)

The AMP version says faith is the title deed. We know a title deed is something that shows two things. One, it shows the item exists even if we do not see it, and, two, it shows who is in possession of it. Faith is a practical expression of your confidence in God and His word. Remember, God and His word are the same. If you have no faith in the word then you have no faith in God. Again, faith is required in order to receive from the kingdom of God. Let's go back to Hebrew 11:6.

> "But without faith it is impossible to please him: for he that cometh to God must believe

that he is, and that he is a rewarder of them that diligently seek him."

Hebrews 11:6

Now let us take a look at the next scripture that should make you feel good in Gods word.

"For we which have believed do enter into rest, as he said, As I have sworn in my wrath, if they shall enter into my rest: although the works were finished from the foundation of the world."

Hebrews 4:3

Faith is not a once in a while thing, it is a way of life. If God was not faithful to His word and His promises, then nobody would believe. We are created in God's image; He lives by faith so we live by faith.

For the Lord is good.
His unfailing love continues forever, and his faithfulness continues to each generation.

Psalm 100:5 (NLT)

This next part is easier said than done, but it is a necessary part of faith. When we go through trials and tribulations, we need to understand that God wants to see how we react. When we are going through trials, do we forget about God, curse God, or praise God? As a Christian, we know the bigger the trial, the bigger the blessing is on the other side of the trial. This is hard to keep straight but when you are going through this trial, and it may be unbearable, you have to keep praising God because the blessing will be that much greater. This might sound contradictory but we should like trials because we know we are in line for a blessing. You may not like it when you are going through it but after it is all over, you will stand and praise God even more than ever.

I use all examples of faith as a tool to help you understand faith. When you are in a relationship, whether the times are good or bad, you need to have a strong foundation of faith (God's word) and rely on God.

Let us dive more into faith. Below, I show the example of Hebrews 11:1 and 11:6. These scriptures are important to remember because faith is how we live.

> Now faith is the substance of things hoped for, the evidence of things not seen.
>
> But without faith it is impossible to please him: for he that cometh to God must believe that he is, and that he is a rewarder of them that diligently seek him.
>
> Hebrews 11:1 & 11:6

The number one thing that will stop your faith is doubt! There are a lot of subsidiary forms of doubt. They come in the form of fear, worrying, anxiety, depression, etc. Circumstances seem to affect people's faith. But we cannot let circumstances affect our faith or our attitude.

One example of faith is in Matthew 5:25–34 where the women with the issue of blood, believed if she just touched Jesus's garment, she would be made whole again. Jesus had not spoken to her at all. She heard he was in the area. Now, you have to remember that at the time Jesus was walking the earth, the New Testament was not written and Jesus had not been crucified yet. Everyone was still under the written law of the Old Testament. In the Old Testament, it was said if a woman had an issue, and her issue in her flesh be blood, she shall be put apart seven days and that no one should touch her for they would be unclean too (Leviticus 15:19–22).

Let us look at what her faith did. It took her from being isolated, not being able to touch anyone, to walking through a crowd where she was most likely touching everyone she passed and then she eventually touched the garment of Jesus. You see she did not even talk to Jesus before she touched his garment. She just said, "If I may touch but his clothes, I shall be whole," and in verse 30, it says, "And Jesus, immediately knowing in himself that virtue had gone out of him." It was by her faith that made her whole.

> And he said unto her, Daughter, thy faith hath made thee whole; go in peace, and be whole of thy plague"
>
> Mathew 5:34

Jesus said "thy faith hath made thee whole," not "touching my clothes has made you whole."

Just to recap this unconditional testimony of faith, this lady had an issue of blood for twelve years. That is roughly 4,384 plus days or 144 months or 624 weeks. This would be a long time for anyone to bare the emotional and psychological distress of being unclean

FAITH: MINI SERMON

and untouchable. When you look at yourself, how many times a day do you have contact with someone?

Her faith made her whole, not the garment. How many other people came out and accidentally bumped into Jesus?

Here, in the next four passages, we see "The just shall live by faith." The *just* can be translated into the "righteous." So, the righteous live by faith. Who are the righteous? The righteous are the people who are saved. The people who have confessed the Lord Jesus Christ is their Lord and savior. The just shall live by faith, the righteous shall live by faith, the saved shall live by faith. Got it? Remember, "But without faith it is impossible to please him," and to further that thought, in Hebrews 10:38, in the second part, it says, "But if any man draw back, my soul shall have no pleasure in him." We know that if the Bible addresses something, it is important. When the Bible addresses something more than once, it is something you should focus on even more.

> Behold, his soul which is lifted up is not upright in him: but the just shall live by his faith.
>
> Habakkuk 2:4

> For therein is the righteousness of God revealed from faith to faith: as it is written, The just shall live by faith.
>
> Romans 1:17

> But that no man is justified by the law in the sight of God, it is evident: for, The just shall live by faith.
>
> Galatians 3:11

> Now the just shall live by faith: but if any man draw back, my soul shall have no pleasure in him.
>
> Hebrews 10:38

Now, let us take a look at the scripture 1 Timothy 6:12 where it says "Fight the good fight of faith." If you look at tough circumstances, we have to have faith. The scripture starts with "fight," meaning that at some point, something will get tough. This has to be recognized because if everything was easy and smooth sailing, you would not have to "fight" and we would not have to have faith. We "fight the good fight" because we are "the just," and "the just" shall live by faith through good and bad circumstances.

Let us look at another test of faith by using the scripture of David and Goliath. Now, one might look at the scriptures of David and Goliath and say how does this pertain to dating? It doesn't, but what it does do is it tells us about a man who has incredible faith in God. No matter what the people told David about Goliath, no matter what they said about his weaponry, no matter what he said about his armor, and no matter what Goliath said to David, David said in total faith "But I come to you in the name of the Lord of Heaven's Armies—the God of the armies of Israel, whom you have defied. Today the Lord will conquer you, and I will kill you and cut off your head" 1 Samuel 17:45–46 (NLT). David did not let circumstances affect his faith. He did not let people's talk affect his decision. By this example alone, you should learn that when circumstances in your relationship are not going right or when you start hearing others talk, you have faith in God. Also, notice that David did not—and I repeat this, did not—say "*I* will conquer you," he said, "*the Lord* will conquer you."

If you relate this to dating then you can look at if someone is trying to talk you out of dating someone because of individual characteristics. When someone says "Why are you dating this person?" they are too short, too tall, too heavy to thin, they don't have the same skin color etc. Then usually they do not have your best interest and are thinking of themselves and what they like. This is also why you should not receive advice coming from the opposite sex especially if they have an interest in you. They will be pointing out or even deliberately make up flaws in the person you like.

A third example of faith is when the centurion believed in Jesus and Jesus healed his servant. If the centurion did not have faith in Jesus and if he did not believe, the healing would not have taken place as you see in Matthew 8:5–13.

The centurion had such great faith in Jesus that he asked Jesus to just speak because he was not worthy to have Jesus come into his home. His faith was unconditional and unwavering. There was not a doubt in his mind that Jesus could not heal his servant from where they were. There was no negotiation between the officer and Jesus, nor any other ritual or transaction. It was by his belief in Jesus alone.

These are three examples of people who had total faith in God and I want to point out they are three totally different situations. It only goes to show that we as Christians should have the same level of faith in

God. It makes God happy when we rely on him. We just need to listen when he speaks, whether it is what we want to hear or not. Faith in not hoping God can do, but knowing He will.

This may sound redundant, but as believers, we have to believe. When you find yourself in a circumstance that the Bible addresses and you say "Yeah, but...," then your belief is not in the word of God. You are only looking at them as just words. When you read scripture, there has to be a belief in your heart. If you say, "Yeah, but it didn't happen for me," then you instantly doubt the word and that is why it does not manifest. If God says it is done, then it is done. That is what you need to wrap your mind around. Remember, the just shall live by faith and faith comes from hearing the word of God (the Bible).

Again, if we are dealing with relationships, if God tells you this is the person for you, then continue regardless of what others say. If God tells you that this is not a match then move on. Do not force it because you will suffer consequences afterward. I am not talking death or illness, but more along the lines of heartbreak. If you are diligently seeking God and he tells you this person is not the one and you keep pressing, God may allow it; but if you do not take his warning signs then the heartbreak will eventually occur. You have to keep the faith because God has someone for you.

NOTES

FASTING

I have mentioned fasting a couple times and would like to communicate my understanding of what fasting is for. There are many ways of fasting. Fasting and prayer are often linked together. Fasting is all about getting closer to God. It is about talking to God and getting answers through prayer. By restricting certain desires, you are showing God you are serious about what you are petitioning Him. It is also important to remember that God knows what you are doing at all times and knows your heart. The book of Acts and Luke records believers fasting before they made important decisions.

> And then was a widow until she was eighty-four. She never left the temple but worshiped night and day, fasting and praying.
>
> Luke 2:37 (NIV)

> They said to him, "John's disciples often fast and pray, and so do the disciples of the Pharisees, but yours go on eating and drinking."
>
> Luke 5:33 (NIV)

> Paul and Barnabas appointed elders for them in each church and, with prayer and fasting, committed them to the Lord, in whom they had put their trust.
>
> Acts 14:23 (NIV)

Fasting is basically taking something that you really like—in some cases crave—and intentionally depriving yourself of it for a period of time. Fasting does not always have to be about food. Other things one might fast from include television, game systems, and hobbies. One thing about fasting is that you have to deprive yourself of things you like and that you will miss. If it does not mean anything to you then it will not mean anything to God.

If you choose to allow your fast to be interrupted then you may not see the same results as if you completed the fast.

When it comes to fasting, we have to put our agenda aside and let God work. Some people fast and try to make God's will conform to their will and they expect to see the result they want to see. Fasting is not is a straight trade, nor will you twist God's arm and make Him change His will. Praise God for all answers, even if it is not what you thought it would be. This is the time to take God's answers and go in that direction. By taking God's answers and following His direction, you are continually praising Him.

It is very important that when you are fasting that you are praying and talking with God on a regular basis. Saying you are going to fast and deprive yourself of food but not seek God's knowledge and answers is called dieting. Depriving yourself of anything without a specific reason is just depriving you of that item and it does not fall into the category of fasting. When you fast, you should be specific about what you are fasting for—whether financial, spiritual, relationships, family, anything, you need to be specific. If you are not specific when you fast, what are you telling God? What will God bless you with or give an answer to?

When you fast, you are seeking God first. The Bible says in Matthew 6:33, "But seek ye first the kingdom of God, and his righteousness; and all these things shall be added unto you." Seeking God first is so important on a daily level because if we seek prosperity first before God, then it is kind of like putting the cart before the horse (it's backward!). Our goal is to seek and find God during a fast.

This is why the support system in the family has to be strong. If a husband says he is hearing from God and needs to fast, the wife needs to support him in the fast. This could be by fasting herself or simply helping with the other entities of the fast. Depending on the type of fast, she may prepare foods that are satisfying to the fast that everyone can eat or make sure the temptations are not there to be seen. Remember, what happens in marriage starts with what happens in your dating lives first. No habits get formed because of marriage. Good fasting habits are always good to start when you are dating.

You can find where the Bible talks about different types of fasting in many chapters. Here are some chapters to reference in fasting, Esther 4, Daniel 10, Leviticus 23, Isaiah 58, and Matthew 4.

FRIENDS AND DATING

This is a topic that has been talked about that does not have a clear-cut answer in the beginning. I have had many discussions on this topic and I feel your views on this topic need to be brought to light with your partner at some point early in the fellowship period. Some feel it is okay to spend time with friends of the opposite sex by themselves when they are dating someone, and some feel that once you start dating, spending time with the opposite sex should be limited to not at all or while they are there. This is an opinionated topic but needs to be discussed early before any attachments start. Who is right? If you have been friends with someone for years before you met your dating partner, should you not be able to spend time with them anymore or do you take the standpoint that you are dating someone and your friend should understand that the dating partner comes first?

FRIENDS AND DATING

Let us start at the point of being married. When you are married, your best friend is your spouse. You should not be spending time or going to lunch or dinner with any other person of the opposite sex saying you are just friends. Remember, when you get married, you are now one, as the scripture says in Genesis 2:23, "Bone of my bones, and flesh of my flesh." So, the question is at what point do you cut back on spending time with your friend of the opposite sex? I feel the easiest answer would be to stop immediately and the friend being a true friend should understand and not take it personally. The most important thing about this is your communication between each other and your feelings. If one person has a standpoint of not spending time with the opposite sex, then the other person either needs to respect that or reevaluate if they want to date this person or be dating at this time. If you put your friends over your relationship, then you will find it hard to stay in a relationship. Regardless of what people say, at some point, there will be the question of why you want to spend so much time with them. At some point, there will be some amount of distrust. This will become evident later in the relationship when you were supposed to be back at a certain time and showed up two hours late. There may have been a good reason, like you were caught in a gridlock traffic jam and could not move, but the distrust will have already started. It may not be your fault but the circumstances are still there. The distrust will also start if at any point when you're married and there is a reduction in the amount of quality time being spent with each other. The initial thought will be of the spouse spending quality time with the other friend. Once that thought process starts, the next process just flows freely, and thoughts of cheating start. There also comes a time when the friend will give a gift and it will be subject to questioning as to why they would get you something like that? If you are looking for a good Christian relationship, then in my opinion, this is one of those things you need to let go of and concentrate on your relationship.

You also have to look at public perception as well. You dating someone and then going and spending time with another person of the opposite sex will be subject to judgment by others. You know it is a platonic friendship, but they may not. It starts gossip going about you. The last thing you want is to find yourself as the topic of conversation with people saying that you are not being faithful to your dating partner. People tend to embellish on the truth. Once people start the gossip of you not being faithful, it will take even more time to develop trust from a good Christian person because they may have heard the gossip. You know it is just gossip but they do not. Is it something that you want to go through?

Some questions that you will want to ask yourself and even have a discussion with your dating partner are:

- Is it appropriate for me to spend time with a friend of the opposite sex if I am dating someone else?
- Is it right for my dating partner to say they do not want me to spend time with a friend that I have known for a long time?

- Am I ready to date if I cannot separate from my friends of the opposite sex?
- Can I be open-minded toward how my dating partner is thinking?
- Do I want to give anyone reason to start talking about me in a negative way?
- What would the consequence be if I did the opposite of what my dating partner believes?
- Am I being selfish by putting a friendship over the potential relationship/marriage?

Can there be extenuating circumstances? Sure.

- You and your partner may have mutual friends that have all been around each other for some time and you have developed the trust between each other that if something comes up, there are no issues. Again, these should still be on the time-limited side.
- You may have your own set of circumstances that will apply only to you and your situation, work, skilled hobby, etc. Just be clear on this subject.

I do advise you to let your dating partner know that you have a friend of the opposite sex in the beginning of your fellowship so it will not be a shock later. There is a trust issue that happens when you introduce a good friend later in the relationship. The question of why didn't you mention them before comes up. Communication is your strongest attribute when it comes to relationships.

PRENUPTIAL AGREEMENTS

As Christians, we have sought God's best for us. A prenuptial agreement is a secular tool put in place based on lack of trust on one person's part. It is put in place in the secular world to retain money and property in the event of a divorce. This does not happen in a Christian marriage. As a Christian we have determined that we can trust this person and that we are bonded for life. Any thought of a prenuptial agreement means there is a lack of trust and that you or the other person is in the flesh and not seeking Gods best for you. This means that you have not developed a solid foundation for marriage and you are taking chances in a secular way.

NOTES

COMPONENTS TO A SUCCESSFUL MARRIAGE

As we look forward toward marriage, I have identified six areas that must be present to keep your marriage going strong. This will be a short chapter due to this being a book on developing the relationship before marriage. There are six elements that need to be present in your relationship in order for it to keep moving strong:

1. Compassion: Compassion is regarded as a fundamental part of human love. Compassion toward your spouse can be explained in a way that when your spouse is going through something you can support them even if you may not understand it. You just help them through it. A primary example is if a woman is having an emotional day and is crying and may not even know why. She may even tell her spouse she does not know why she is so emotional. It

COMPONENTS TO A SUCCESSFUL MARRIAGE

is up to the husband to have compassion for her and what she is going though. Anything less may seem insensitive to her and may even cause an argument.

2. Companionship: A commitment to fulfill your God-ordained marriage responsibility to your wife or husband. What does that mean? You need to spend time with your spouse. They are your best friend! This is spending time at home as well as going out and spending time with each other. You will want to do things that brought you together as well as try new things as a married couple. When you try new things, it is called life enrichment. Doing the same old, same old gets redundant and you will lose interest and the relationship becomes boring. One way is to take a vacation somewhere where you can see God made beautiful. Take a cruise where you can visit a few islands in one vacation. Sometimes, just the planning and looking up places to go to is a fun thing to do. It is the part of sharing time with each other.

3. Romance: An expressive and pleasurable feeling from an emotional attraction to another person associated with love. Romance is the deep and strong emotional desires to connect with another person intimately. It is important because it is what brings both husband and wife together to express love to each other that cannot be expressed with others around.

4. Commitment: Being bound emotionally and intellectually to another person. When you are dating and you form a commitment with that person, you are saying they are the only person for you and that you are no longer looking for anyone else. This is a verbal and physical commitment. Your final commitment is when you say "I do." This is a commitment not just to you and your spouse but also to the Lord. It is now a covenant.
5. Passion: How much you want something and the drive you have to keep it or get it. An example of someone who has a passion for something would be a head football coach. The head football coach knows offensive plays and defensive plays. He also understands strategy and can find strong points and week points on the opposing team. He has a drive that makes him spend countless hours studying film learning about the other team. Then he also looks at his own team and can identify the strengths and the weaknesses of his own team and what they need to do to get better. He knows statistics and the odds of something working or not. A good coach is serious about football and does not treat it like a part-time holiday job. He is passionate about football.

The same needs to be applied to your relationship. You should want to keep learning about your partner's strengths and weaknesses. You should also be looking at yourself to be able to identify your strengths and weaknesses and try to improve on them as well. Passion is a strong driving force and you need to apply it in your relationship. If your partner loves to receive gifts, keep them happy by giving them gifts that they like and can use. If your partner loves it when you do something nice for them, then keep that on the forefront of your mind. Learn what your partner likes and apply it to your relationship. When it comes to marriage, you should be passionate about the marriage and every facet of what marriage entails. A marriage cannot be treated like a part-time holiday job. There has to be passion in the relationship to keep moving the marriage forward.

6. Transparency: This is a part of your relationship that implies openness. Everyone has habits they may do in private that may not be suitable for doing around others. One example would be you would not go over to a friend's house and lounge around in your boxers the way you would at home. Transparency is being completely comfortable around this other person not trying to hold back who you are when you are married. This would follow the scripture in Genesis 2:25.

> And they were both naked, the man and his wife, and were not ashamed.
>
> Genesis 2:25 (KJV)

There are some of us that know people who have been married for thirty plus years. It is important that you are not trying to imitate their marriage. There is a saying that goes like this: "We do not seek to imitate our mentors yet we seek what they have already sought." Imitating a marriage only lasts so long because you do not know what other couples have gone through to get to where they are today. You can take advice from them but your marriage has to be unique to you. Nobody will have the same marriage because everyone is different and has different circumstances. You can take what they tell you and learn from them but inevitably your marriage is unique.

NOTES

FUSION OF MARRIAGE

Now that we have established all of the processes, timelines, person and their vision, we enter into an engagement to be married. Still, through the engagement, you should be learning about each other. This is a time to disclose anything that you need to that may be on a more sensitive side. It is a time to talk that if it is brought up at a later time by someone else, it will not be a surprise and an issue that will cause a disruption in the marriage. As Christians, we try to do everything we can to learn about this person so when we say "I do," it means for good, not for right now. If there are parts of your past that you did not want to disclose because you were afraid of being judged by the person, now is the time to do so. You do not want or need someone bringing up your past to your spouse and have it be a devastating shock and have it affect your marriage.

FUSION OF MARRIAGE

For this reason, you need to look at marriage in a different way. I am going to start with a math question. One plus one equals two, right? Yes, but not always. In high school, I heard a physics teacher say they can make one plus one is equal to one. I said how is that, it does not make sense. He said it does when you deal with fusion. Apparently, he thought I understood that but didn't explain. It was not until I heard my pastor break it down into simple terms that I understood it. For example, if you mix yellow and blue together, you get green. One yellow plus one blue equals one green. You do not look at the green and say, "Look, there are two parts, yellow and blue together," because you cannot see the yellow or blue anymore. They have been fused together to form one color—green. It is the same with God. One Father, one Son, and one Holy Spirit equal one God. They are separate, but fused together in one God. So let us go back to the beginning of man with Adam. Adam was formed out of the dust of the earth. Could God have created Eve from the earth as well? Sure, he could have. But God chose to take a rib from Adam and form Eve so the two could be fused back into one body. "And Adam said, This is now bone of my bones, and flesh of my flesh: she shall be called Woman, because she was taken out of Man." One body, one covenant, one God! Marriage is the fusion of man and woman back together into one body. Not physically but spiritually. This is why, as Christians, we need to have a solid foundation, a foundation that is built on our love for God, trust, life experiences, our ability to communicate with one another, and our common interests.

With all that said, I pray that you find God's best for you and utilize the knowledge in this book to help create a solid foundation for your marriage. I pray that the next time you say "I do" is the last time you say it and it lasts a lifetime.

NOTES

EFFECTS OF DIVORCE

When God created the earth, He created a perfect planet. He created marriage to be a divine institution. Divorce was created by man as a way to be free from their spouse. As you see in Matthew 19:8, it was never a way of God or in his will. God is very clear in Malachi 2:16 about His views on divorce. He did not intend for divorce to be part of His perfect planet just like murder, stealing, or adultery. God never commands divorce. Jesus says the only time divorce is allowed biblically is in Matthew 5:31-32 and then reminds us of our commitment to our vows in 5:33.

> Jesus replied, "Moses permitted divorce only as a concession to your hard hearts, but it was not what God had originally intended."
>
> Matthew 19:8 (NLT)

EFFECTS OF DIVORCE

> "For I hate divorce!" says the Lord, the God of Israel. "To divorce your wife is to overwhelm her with cruelty," says the Lord of Heaven's Armies. "So guard your heart; do not be unfaithful to your wife."
>
> Malachi 2:16 (NLT)

> "You have heard the law that says, 'A man can divorce his wife by merely giving her a written notice of divorce. But I say that a man who divorces his wife, unless she has been unfaithful, causes her to commit adultery. And anyone who marries a divorced woman also commits adultery. "You have also heard that our ancestors were told, 'You must not break your vows; you must carry out the vows you make to the Lord.
>
> Matthew 5:31-33 (NLT)

Anytime a divorce happens, you can point to sin or a selfish desire on the part of one or both people. As many reasons why you think there should be grounds for divorce, there is only one biblically (adultery). It doesn't matter if you fell out of love, you do not get along anymore, it does not matter if your spouse turns to drinking, drugs, spends too much time on their hobbies, loses their job, sleeps too much, does not do anything around the house, can't cook, or whatever else you complain about. These things are dealt with through prayer and petition (fasting).

As a Christian, you have to understand that love never fails. You should not look at love as being a weak attribute. Remember, in the "What Is Love" section, we learned that love is the strongest of faith, hope, and love. When you put the love for things (hobbies, sports, money, business, etc.) first in front of your marriage, then the love in your marriage becomes weak. Love is never weak. It is our selfish desires that takes over and makes love appear weak. When that sin or selfish desire takes place of love, then it is easier to see the world's way out through divorce.

On the grounds of an abusive relationship, the Bible does not say you cannot separate. Getting away from the abuse and trying to resolve the problems and getting the person help is more recommended than divorce.

Divorce starts a trend. Once most people do it and they survive physically, they instantly get conditioned that if they marry again they will just get another divorce if it does not work out. Trying to make it work turns into divorce much faster. The divorce statistics prove it. The average statistic for divorce among first marriages is 50 percent, 60 percent for second marriages, and up to 73 percent for a third marriage. What the divorce statistics don't show is how the immediate family is affected by the divorce or how the extended families are hurt by the divorce. It doesn't show the division of friends or how the children are affected either. The statistics don't show how your children's attitudes change, their grades drop, even the emotional changes of anger or depression.

EFFECTS OF DIVORCE

You should always try to resurrect your marriage even if you think it is over. Fighting for your marriage is best for you and your family and sets an example for your children not to give up if they have a difficult time in their marriage.

FINAL WORDS

This book was designed to help you identify characteristics in people and even understand yourself better. As a word of knowledge, your friendship should flow with the other person. If you are fighting to keep a relationship together in the first week, two, or even a month, then you are not equally yoked. You are trying to force something that is not there which means you are in the flesh.

It is important to also understand that if it appears that someone is only giving you half effort while you are dating then they will only give you half an effort when you are married. You shouldn't want to settle for anything less than God's best for you.

I believe if you date one person at a time, you will understand that person faster and determine if you are equally yoked or not. You need to put all your efforts into one relationship at a time. If you date several people at a time, it is difficult to give someone or any one of them your all when it has to be divided over several people. It becomes harder to determine what you want because everyone has "a certain something" that you can find that you like about them. One person may have a better body, one person may have a better personality, one person may be more helpful than another, one person may be more giving than another, etc. So, who do you pick when they all have good qualities? It just makes the process much longer to find the right person.

I would also like to encourage you to enjoy dating. Enjoy spending time together and planning things together. Don't rush the dating process to get married. Many people rush the dating process to get to the sex part. They want to be in the will of God when they have sex. When you are dating, you are trying to find a life partner. Enjoy your dating experience. You will thank and glorify God that you did.

Marriage is a lifelong covenant. It takes time and effort to keep it working smoothly. Marriage is a team effort. There's the old saying "There is no 'I' in team." Decisions need to be made for the family, not for the sake of one person.

The most important thing to remember is your relationship with God. He wants us to rely on Him. He is worthy and capable of anything and everything.

I would like to wish you and your significant other the very best of what God has to offer you. I pray the Lord will bless you and your partner so that you may never surrender to whatever challenges that come your way. I pray your hearts are filled with love for each other and that you realize each other's worth. I pray you are not led into temptations and that you let God guide you wherever you go in Jesus's name. Amen.